ANY GIVEN TEAM

Ray McLean taught physical education in country Victoria for eight years before joining the Royal Australian Air Force where he was assigned to redesigning leadership and teamwork training at the Airman Aircrew Flying Training School. He left the RAAF in 1994 to establish his own training consultancy, adapting performance improvement principles to sport and business. He is currently the Director of Training for Leading Teams and lives in Ballarat with his wife and three children.

Any Given Team

Improving Leadership and Team Performance

RAY McLEAN

A PAUL G. CONROY BOOK for
LEADING TEAMS
PO Box 450
North Melbourne VIC 3051
Phone: (03) 9326 6889
Email: info@leadingteams.net.au
www.leadingteams.net.au

National Library of Australia
Cataloguing-in-Publication entry

McLean, Ray J., 1959—

Any Given Team: Improving Leadership and Team Performance

ISBN 0 9775038 0 1.

1. Leadership. 2. Teams in the workplace.
3. Teamwork (Sports). I. Conroy, Paul. II. Title.

658.4022

Contents

For Sally, Courtney, Jackson and Jesse,
who let me chase a dream

Preface

GENERALLY I'D START A WORKSHOP with the question, 'What did you expect to learn by coming here?' Before you read the following chapters, I'd like you to think about that question. What are you hoping to learn from this book? Learning something is so utterly different to being taught it. Learning, as Einstein said, is what's left when you have forgotten all you have been taught.

Some years ago I saw a cartoon that to me illustrated perfectly the gulf that exists between learning and teaching. Featuring Stripe the dog and some young boys, Stripe's master says proudly, 'I taught Stripe to whistle'. His friends cock their ears and listen and wait … Eventually one of the boys says, 'I can't hear anything'. Stripe's owner, still looking pleased with himself, replies, 'Oh no, I only taught him. He didn't learn anything.'

That distinction between teaching and learning has been central to my thinking for the fifteen years that I've been involved in leadership and teamwork development training and it remained so when I sat down to write this book. On the one hand, I wanted to share some of the experiences I've had working with individuals and teams and to introduce readers to some ideas they might not have previously considered for improving individual and team performances. On the other, what would be the best way to relate what I learned without resorting to dry lists of principles, guidelines and rules? Because what would the reader be left with when they put *that* book down? What would they have learned? Would they even read it?

In the end I rejected the impersonal version, and not just because it's a dull way to look at what I recall as being full of colour and movement, intriguing personalities and some unforgettable odours, but because whenever I've learned anything it has been from being around people.

When I first tried to write a book on what I've learned I didn't go back far enough or in enough detail, wanting to avoid, perhaps, the impression that I was presuming to be writing an autobiography. So skirting the names and places seemed like a good idea at the time. But the results tended towards a textbook, and a not very useful one at that. As a diagram and checklists the framework doesn't do a lot, not without people in it. More illuminating, I think, is a simple retelling of how the framework evolved among people and from real situations and how it has been adapted and successfully applied to other situations.

At workshops and sessions I've attended people are sometimes curious to know how I came across a particular idea or, more broadly, how I ever came to be in a position to be developing a framework with applications across so many areas. The usual constraints—time, time and time—have often meant recounting abbreviated versions of events but, thankfully, not for often or long enough to have forgotten what really happened.

Much of the work I do now to help improve individual and team performance is based firmly on what was learned along the way, about how I and others behaved in particular circumstances and why we behaved the way we did. In that sense, the programs for individuals and teams now being implemented by businesses, sports teams and other groups really do have their origins in north-central

Victoria in the mid-1980s, me pushing a pram about the backstreets of a country town, ambivalent about my work and anxious for the future.

The people and organisations named in the text played significant roles in developing a model increasingly being identified by business, education and sporting organisations across Australia and internationally as their favoured model for improving team performances. How many of those perched in skyscrapers or working out in four-tier stadiums would recognise that parts of the model they are following were devised over a few beers in the South Australian dust and developed among weekend footballers in draughty corrugated iron sheds in northern and western Victoria? I sincerely hope the individuals I name, as well many others I don't— they will know who they are—appreciate just how significant their roles were in setting the foundations for the burgeoning field based on the principles they helped devise.

As I discuss in the main text, books and overhead transparencies are, so far as learning goes, inferior substitutes for getting out there and actually doing it; no book, this or any other, is going to transform readers into great leaders or make them the ultimate team players. That takes practice.

When you put the book down I hope you'll have some new ideas—perhaps even some new attitudes—to put into practice for your own improvement and for the improvement of the teams you work in or lead.

RJM
Ballarat, 2006

Foreword

After a season as senior coach with the Central District Football Club in the South Australian National Football League, I realised that if we were going to be successful there needed to be significant changes in the way the club and the team approached their football. Ray McLean outlined his program to me and how it might change the club's culture. Importantly, he said it would need time— probably two to three seasons—for the change to take place.

I'd always seen it as a coach's responsibility to enforce discipline, implement game plans and tactics, demand higher standards and motivate the team and the individuals in it. With Ray's program, I had to adjust to the team having much more input to what happened both on and off the field. At times it was confronting and there were casualties along the way but it did create a healthy environment where everyone at the club had a clear understanding of what had to be done to win the respect of the football community. Above all, the program taught me the importance of the team as a powerful resource in the quest to produce the best outcomes.

Alan Stewart
Adelaide Crows Football Club

I was introduced to Ray McLean at our football club where he facilitated some sessions on what we wanted out of the season and how we wanted to be seen as a team. Soon afterwards he conducted a training camp where there were no particular rules about how we spent our free time. Afterwards, with Ray's help, we honestly reviewed our behaviour and compared it with what we'd said at the earlier session. I hadn't experienced anything like it before and sensed immediately what a powerful learning process it was. The team then decided on a set of behaviours and values that we agreed to live by. The team culture improved as we took ownership of our behaviour and the results eventually followed.

Robert Harvey
St Kilda Football Club

Some years ago at Monash University we asked Ray McLean to develop a leadership program for our students. We found his insights into leadership, learning, self-awareness and teamwork so useful that we then ran the program as executive leadership team development for the university's commercial enterprise, Monyx. Our business results have improved and others using Ray's approach are reporting similar successes.

Ray describes it as learning to be 'fair dinkum'; simply, being honest with yourself and others. His direct, no-nonsense approach shows how honesty, learning and leadership are interconnected and how they apply to you whether you're leading a company with thousands of employees, a sporting team or a family.

Andrew O'Brien
Monyx Pty Ltd, Melbourne

As I got to the end of my playing days I started to question the structures of football clubs. Why don't players have more say in the running of their team? As a coach I was determined to give the players more input.

I realised when I was introduced to Ray McLean that I'd found the perfect ally. It has been a very good association, one that has been valued and embraced by players and staff alike. His impact over the three years has been significant, culminating in the Swans winning the 2005 Australian Football League premiership.

The culture at our football club is one we are all proud of and one we have worked very hard to achieve. The players deserve most of the credit as it has been primarily driven by them. However, it would not have been achieved without Ray's direction and guidance.

Paul Roos
Sydney Swans Football Club

Ray McLean is expert in assisting organisations develop their culture and values. An outstanding facilitator and communicator, he emphasises the importance of individuals taking responsibility and becoming leaders to achieve better team performance.

Brian Goorjian
Sydney Kings Basketball Club

INTRODUCTION

I FIRST THOUGHT SERIOUSLY about writing a book when I was described in a daily newspaper as the 'mystery man' a football club had called in, the insinuation being I didn't want to be identified or my work revealed. That journalist must have lost my business card.

Other times the job title has been 'leadership trainer' and 'teamwork facilitator'—which are close to the mark and ones I tend to use—and, less accurately, 'human resources consultant', 'motivator', 'careers counsellor', 'sports psychologist', 'player development manager', 'life coach', 'mentor' and 'cultural change manager'. Once I was introduced to a large and influential audience as an 'industrial psychologist' and, as I told the handful who stayed behind to hear more, I don't call myself that either. Nor am I the 'ex-SAS commando' that I was said to be in some newspaper reports.

Whenever I come home from working with the Sydney Swans or Adelaide Crows in the Australian Football League or the Waratahs in Rugby Union Super 14 or the St George Illawarra Dragons in the National Rugby League, my children always ask me with a good deal of interest, 'How did you go?' But underneath that enthusiasm I'm not sure even they understand what it is I actually do.

So—and readers not blessed with children may want to skip to the next paragraph because they might not understand—this book is also a father's attempt to explain to his kids why he's been away so often, particularly on weekends, and why they've been dragged along to so many different sports events in far-flung places and missed *Simpsons* repeats. It's a selfish motive but one I hope, in time, they might appreciate (if not before I'm gone, which would be better again.)

The following chapters won't be coming up with any better two- or three-word job titles I should be using but they might shed enough light on the work itself for readers to conclude like me that it isn't particularly important what you call it so long as you know what it is.

Given the heavy media coverage of some sports in Australia it's only to be expected that it's my work with high-profile sports teams that generates the most curiosity, even though it's essentially the same work I do with business groups, municipal workers and schoolkids.

That across-the-board interest in sport works in my favour in a few ways. If it's sport that gets people interested in what I do in the first place, then sport is also a good backdrop to explain how a performance improvement framework operates in practice. And more people are familiar with sporting scenarios than just about any other teamwork situation I know of so there's generally fewer whys and wherefores about the team's purpose.

Plus, and it's a significant plus, people tend to be more receptive to hearing how athletes improved their performances ahead of, say, parking officers, debt collectors or snake breeders. In that regard, my recollections of some interesting and rewarding experiences at Collingwood Football Club might have made for marginally better reading had my Essendon-supporting editor been willing to look at them.

~

I WAS FIRST PROPERLY INTRODUCED to concepts of teamwork and leadership in 1991 while working as an education officer in the Royal Australian Air Force. At that stage our approach to leadership training was largely theoretical, with overly optimistic expectations that this inherently practical skill could be taught within a classroom. We lectured students about leadership, they sat an exam and those exam results supposedly rated their leadership abilities. How the students went thereafter applying the theories, if at all, to real situations was at best a secondary consideration. It was like teaching students the underlying physics of the bicycle and saying, as they emerged blinking into the sunlight and wobbling all over the road, that we'd developed—overlooking for the moment their complete lack of riding experience—top cyclists.

So how could we best teach leadership? It was only after we stripped away our preconceptions and began asking the students that we began to make some headway into the problem.

As we were to learn, any given group—in fact, any given individual—already knew the answers. But they knew it intuitively, not as theory. Everyone had seen it and said they'd recognise it if they saw it again. But describe it?

Like their instructors, they struggled to put it into words. And whenever it seemed to have been roughly articulated, those words were little if any guidance in even slightly different situations. There were more exceptions than rules. Eventually we gave up trying to define leadership in words and that was a giant leap forward.

Leadership is action. If you can do it, the theory is largely superfluous. And if you can't do it, the theory is still superfluous.

As close as we ever got to a description of a leader that could be applied across the board to all sorts of situations was someone who, upon realising something was amiss in a particular situation, tried to do something about it. Leaders see something and they do something. They act.

We gave the students some rudimentary instructions and handed them—figuratively speaking—bikes, a destination and a map and let them get on with it while we observed them in action. And when they'd finished we finally had something to talk about.

Afterwards, when we asked questions like, 'What do you think a good leader does?' or 'When you have finished this course, what sort of behaviours should you be displaying as a highly effective leader?' the responses were authentic, not red-faced suppositions or parroted theories dressed up as knowledge. We'd stopped talking theory and talked about what happened in a common language based on a shared experience.

We soon learned—irrespective of their theoretical grounding, age, rank, physique, gender or any of the other presumptions that often colour leadership judgments—who the real leaders were. With the students setting their own criteria for leadership we redesigned the training to reflect that. No longer would we tell students what leadership was in theory, we would let them work it out among themselves.

Significantly, we also changed the assessment criteria and began to rely more on peer evaluations to gauge the development of leaders. We were learning not only who the real leaders were, we were inadvertently learning how people wanted to be led to feel they'd been led effectively.

It was a different approach and, as the results were surely indicating, extraordinarily effective.

As I continued to develop the leadership and team training with the airmen aircrew personnel I became committed to the idea that the principles and the model we were developing would be applicable to any team.

~

IN EARLY 1993 WE BEGAN a pilot program involving the Central District Football Club that changed the focus and direction of my career irrevocably. The team's improved performances created some interest among the club's corporate partners in the team-building and cultural-change programs we were developing. We oriented the framework to the corporate objectives and found, as I'd suspected, that the principles applied in business environments as well.

As those programs developed and the athletes we were working with developed their leadership and teamwork skills, one thing led to another and the athletes took to the platform and began running the programs themselves. From there Leading Teams was born, an organisation run by athletes to deliver a range of team development and life-skills programs to other athletes, corporate teams and community groups, as well as supporting athletes while they are participants then providing them with a career option afterwards.

As I write, a team of trained athlete-facilitators are running the kinds of programs I used to run in schools, football clubs and business and community groups. How well is it working? I like to think that Leading Teams has the potential to change Australian sport and the Australian workplace for the better but the jury is going to be out on that one for a while yet. All I know for sure is that my life and workplace have changed for the better and I've derived enormous satisfaction from watching the athletes and the business grow to the point that it's now a sustainable operation whether I turn up or not. Leading Teams will comfortably outlast its founders and in years to come athletes entering the organisation might well wonder how it all started way back in the twentieth century.

Over the last few years the performance improvement programs have been successfully applied by numerous business, educational and community organisations, as well as at the Sydney, Adelaide, St Kilda, North Melbourne and Collingwood football clubs in the Australian Football League, St George Illawarra in the National Rugby League, the Waratahs in the

Rugby Union Super 14, the Sydney Kings and the Wollongong Hawks in the National Basketball League, the Australian national basketball teams, the Boomers and the Opals, and the Australian women's wheelchair basketball team, the Gliders.

Readers familiar with those teams' performances in recent times might have detected some subtle similarities in the way those teams go about their work, and how they've often surprised observers with their improved performances. There's no smoke and mirrors involved, though I suspect some folk might find it more believable if there were.

The simple truth is that the individuals in those teams have all worked incredibly hard and made extraordinary sacrifices to help their team, and they didn't choose between working harder or working smarter. They worked harder *and* smarter.

Promoting as we do a behaviour-based performance improvement framework, there's perhaps an assumption that I must have a vested interest in promoting 'honesty' and that the model we've devised stems from some unsaid motivation to do good. Nonsense. If people and teams performed better in a dishonest, deceitful environment, I wouldn't hesitate to pass that on either. But I've yet to see it.

The following chapters are, I hope, an easy-to-read introduction to the principles behind what's become known as the Leading Teams Performance Improvement Program and offers readers some insights into how those principles originated and work in practice.

WHAT'S WRONG WITH THIS PICTURE?

NOT LONG AGO I DROPPED INTO A BANK for what I'd planned to be a couple of minutes. It wasn't reckless optimism; everything was in place for a quick getaway. There were three staff and, counting me, one customer.

Just inside the entrance there was a big sign about the bank's vision, mission and values. Being in the vision-mission-values industry myself and, with the three staff huddled in earnest discussion, I stopped to see if there was anything in the sign worth appropriating for the business, and to give them a few seconds to finish their conversation rather than, I suppose, just barging in on them. The sign on the wall said, and I paraphrase here, that in all creation, nothing is more important to this bank than its customers; that customers cause the sun to shine and birds to sing, and; only the gullible would trust their money elsewhere.

I went back over to the famously eager-to-please staff. A few metres away, backs to me, they kept talking. I went back over to the vision-mission-values sign to see I'd read it right the first time. They didn't react. They were oblivious, or so it seemed. But I've heard bank staff are always vigilant and particularly so at quiet times. They knew I was there.

Were they really so deep in discussion they couldn't serve me? In their minds, if I were convinced they were engaged in a crucial discussion then they weren't actually declining a customer service. But each of them would have been looking intently at the others, not quite sure of themselves, and thinking, 'Well, if these two are behaving as if this is okay, then it's surely okay for me to do it too?' That's culture—if enough people are doing it then it must be okay—and it can legitimise some unusual behaviour. Norm doesn't mean normal.

The only message I'd got in the bank so far was that—and it's one we get so regularly I think we cease to even acknowledge it to ourselves—I was *just* a customer in this environment and customers wait. That message wasn't on the sign but it was loud and clear.

I knew now why the bank had opted for such a large sign; the customers weren't going to be shown the bank's values by its staff's behaviour so the customers would have to be told, and as loudly as possible.

One of the staff looked over my way and rescue seemed imminent but they turned away again. That unsaid message was, 'I've seen you, I'm busy, now wait.' I thought about removing— well, tearing—the vision-mission-values sign off the wall and placing—well, sticking—it where it was most needed. I moved back towards the sign.

'You right there?'

I'd become irritating enough to warrant being seen to. I played that game as a kid—you're given what you want to be rid of you.

Thick carpet, cleverly worded signs about charters, missions and the best of intentions are the talk. The walk is serving customers to get rid of them.

Who knows what these bank staff were really thinking? The only message I got, the only verifiable cause-and-effect that registered in whatever part of my brain that catalogues these things, was from their behaviour. That is, from what they did and what I saw.

So, given the staff's behaviour, how should I behave to get what I want from the situation? In this case I'd logged for future reference that at this bank I am a bug that'll be rewarded with more attentive service when I look irritated and angry and make a nuisance of myself.

~

THEIR VISION-MISSION-VALUES statement was looking a bit like a STOP sign that no one stops at anymore because, well, no one stops there anymore. And if anyone did now it'd probably cause an accident because no one else would be expecting it. The sign is past useless now, it just adds to the confusion.

But there's nothing actually wrong with the sign, it's just some well-intended advice for avoiding trouble a bit further down the road. No one expects a STOP sign to operate their brakes or turn off their engine. Drivers see STOP and—if they get the message and know what to do with it—they take their foot off the accelerator, squeeze the brakes, clutch in, shift down, clutch out, more brake, clutch in, shift down, clutch out, etc., until they eventually stop.

I'm not sure there's a similar understanding that declarations about visions, missions and values are only signs and that a series of actions—behaviours—are required to make good of the information. How would these staff go if their three-hundred-word core-values statement were like the STOP sign and they had to weigh up its advice and then act on it. How would they go there? ... INTEGRITY ... UNSWERVING COMMITMENT ... LOYALTY ... COMMUNITY ... HONESTY ... How would they do those because the sign certainly doesn't say how? And if they did know what to do and how to do it but others weren't doing it, would they do it anyway?

Signs don't do anything. They pass on some information that might help a difficult situation, that's all. But if people don't know what to make of the information, if they don't know what to do, then how's that sign's message going to change anything? People have to know *what* to do, *how* to do it and then, above all, have a culture of actually *doing* it. If any one of those components is missing, then behaviour can't change and nothing changes. *Nothing* changes.

What would these bank staff do at the STOP sign that no one stops at? Would they obey it? Or have the common sense to just go straight through like everyone else? Maybe they'd slow to a crawl and claim they were the best of a bad lot? Would they arrange for the sign's removal or, alternatively, argue in favour of getting a bigger sign made?

Or, would one of them have the courage to state the obvious? There's nothing wrong with the sign. The problem is their behaviour.

~

IT'S USUALLY ONLY A MINOR INCONVENIENCE when teams don't operate effectively, as it was for me at the bank.

Now, I don't know a lot about how a bank works. But I imagine there are all sorts of teams in there beavering away on various projects, all designed to make it better for the people who work there and patronise its halls as customers and invest in its stocks. I'm not sure how well it's working out for them because I don't know how you properly measure a bank's performance. The bank I was in made millions of dollars in profits last year. So they're probably better at it than I think they are. But I'll bet they're not as good at it as they think they are.

What I do know is that banking is a fairly soft form of competition compared to some other arenas I'm familiar with.

No Destination, No Direction

One lesson I learned the hard way is that playing it safe isn't always sensible or, for that matter, even safe. My first shot at career fulfilment was teaching secondary school physical education which, looking back, was a logical rather than particularly well-considered decision.

Schools were a fixture in my life long before I ever attended one as a student; my father was a primary school teacher who, by the time he died, had taught for thirty-seven years, and most of those in one- and two-teacher schools dotted around the backblocks of north-western Victoria. We lived in Education Department houses that were more often than not right beside the schools, and the classrooms, playgrounds and sports fields next door were very much an extension of the family home.

If my feeling comfortable around school environs was one criterion for going on to teaching, I'd met it. But if that was a factor, it was still nowhere near as significant as the impact my father's approach to teaching and the satisfaction he got from it had on me. He enjoyed teaching immensely and he did it extremely well. Everything he said and did as a teacher was measured against the learning outcomes and if he couldn't see the learning he couldn't see the point. If that put him, if not at odds with, then on a different trajectory to the education establishment, his solution was teaching in small, remote schools where he could be as autonomous as possible within a sprawling regimented bureaucracy.

I was one of his pupils for four years when he was literally the only teacher in town, and he was as effective in the classroom as he was at home in making sense of ideas and arguments in a few memorable words. No one in his class got left behind, he always had another way of putting it until everyone, eventually, knew what they needed to know. It was like he carried a huge set of keys with him and if the door didn't open with this one he'd move straight on to the next one, and if that didn't work, the one after that. His classes ploughed through the work.

~

OUT THERE SPORT WAS THE ONLY community activity to speak of and any Wimmera–Mallee locality worth its own name had a paddock set aside as a football ground, a malthoid cricket pitch in the middle and a cluster of asphalt netball courts and tennis courts around the edges. Over summer we played competitive tennis, travelling to other semi-remote locations that were sometimes represented by three generations of the one family.

But, being south of the Murray River, summer sports were essentially a way to pass time until the next footy season rolled around.

Australian football introduced itself to me in the shape of farmers, publicans and schoolteachers slugging it out in mud and icy rain, me watching from behind a misty car windscreen. The

Victorian Football League broadcasts fading in and out on the car radio put the rough and tumble matches we were witnessing into their proper context; this game could take you all the way to the Melbourne Cricket Ground where matches were played in front of a hundred thousand spectators.

Like any other kid living south of the Murray River in the 1960s I had a loose plan to play a couple of hundred outstanding VFL games for Richmond. So I played football the first chance I had and found out sooner rather than later what a hard game it is.

Junior football was an introduction of sorts to the rudiments of team-building and performance-improvement ideas. Coaches took their lead from high-profile VFL coaches and delivered passionate rants during the breaks, starting out as a reasoned whisper begging the players to lift, then telling them to go in harder, and then demanding they jump higher, run faster and be stronger and more skilful and to fight them on the beaches, in the fields and in the streets and to never ... ever ... surrender. It was terrific theatre.

The change-rooms were invariably decked out with slogans: A CHAMPION TEAM BEATS A TEAM OF CHAMPIONS ... WHEN THE GOING GETS TOUGH THE TOUGH GET GOING ... ALL FOR ONE AND ONE FOR ALL ... THERE IS NO 'I' IN TEAM. I can remember thinking after yet another flogging that if vaudevillian coaching and cleverly worded signs were improving our performance it couldn't have been by much because, it was generally agreed, as a team we couldn't have gone any worse than we already were. And, as I learned when I first played senior football as a fifteen-year-old and had a beer can thrust into my hand as a rite of passage, the Foster's-enhanced team-bonding sessions didn't help either.

~

SECONDARY EDUCATION WAS INTERESTING, a boys school with around seven hundred students guided by sixty or so staff with competing and often conflicting teaching philosophies. Some teachers were openly saying to anyone who'd listen, including the students, that there were problems with the school. Some thought they could improve the school by talking it down, others by talking it up. There was always plenty of talk.

But it was only background noise. The school had football ovals, basketball and volleyball courts and a gymnasium, and the town, population just under ten thousand, might have been preparing to host its own summer Olympics since it had the facilities for every sport I'd ever heard of, plus a few I hadn't. I had a go at all of them. A drive-in movie theatre and a cinema looked after teenage nightlife and, being on the highway between Melbourne and Adelaide, there was a steady supply of touring rock bands so we could lose the top end of our hearing just like the city kids.

At school I was forming opinions on teaching styles and how they related to learning because it was too obvious that some of them had no relationship to it at all. There were teachers— veterans and novices alike—whose 'method' was writing on blackboards in silence for hour after hour while students furiously copied it all down in their exercise books.

Others saw teaching as an exercise in verbal or physical intimidation, as if dread was a condition for learning. It was enough of a challenge working out what we were meant to be learning from some of them, let alone actually learning it. And there was always a contingent of teachers so homesick for the city that teaching was mainly a hungover afterthought.

With so many of the teaching staff unhappy or not wanting to be there, it must have been a struggle for all of them. Yet the committed teachers were still getting their messages across, turning up keen and prepared and, I thought, feeling sufficiently rewarded by the work to make it worthwhile doing it well. Those teachers and the way they went about it had an impact on me.

I never enjoyed the so-called 'academic demands', the ones that didn't feel like learning to me, though I usually coped with them. Secondary school really paid off for me with the social and sporting opportunities it presented. There was always someone to share whatever your interests were and it was never a problem getting enough people together for a ball game.

Sometime during year 11 or 12 I began to realise secondary school wouldn't actually go on forever. I looked at my father and thought, well, he seemed happy in what he was doing. And I couldn't remember a time when I hadn't looked forward to being at school, and I was fascinated by sport. Teaching physical education seemed to fit the bill.

I recall parents and teachers saying to me to think very, very carefully about my career choice—as they do, because they invariably hadn't—and me reassuring them that I most certainly had. After all, I'd quietly abandoned my earlier plan to be a professional footballer and I thought that showed some maturity of thought. But rather than actively choosing teaching I probably chose it because I hadn't chosen anything else.

I've often wondered about my family's connection to teaching and how it affected my thinking. My younger brother—same parents, same houses, the same schools—didn't think much of his schooldays at the time and preferably not at all nowadays. Perhaps that was his destiny, once his older brother had occupied the contrary position?

~

I WAS ADMITTED into the secondary physical education course at the then Ballarat College of Advanced Education in 1977. I got through those four years without blazing any trails academically, that's for sure, but I thoroughly enjoyed the experience. There's probably a book in those four years but it would be a different kind of book to this, except the part where, at a typically raucous student party, I set eyes upon my future wife, Sally, and we go on to live happily ever after.

Like secondary school, I just kept on keeping on until teachers' college eventually drew to an end and they handed me a degree and sent me back to a secondary school. In early 1981 I was posted to Donald, a town of fifteen hundred people in north-central Victoria. I was familiar with the country town lifestyle, revolving as it did around the schools, sports clubs and hotels, and I'd have had no complaints whatsoever if Sally hadn't been posted to Stawell, an hour's drive south. After my two years of 'independent living', the Department took one look at the shape I was in and forthwith transferred Sally to Donald on compassionate grounds.

I can only try to imagine what Donald must have looked like to Sally, who'd grown up in a leafy Melbourne suburb surrounded by rolling hills and millions of people. Donald is not like that. On the flanks of Lake Buloke, a wetland known for hosting confrontations between duck shooters, animal rights protesters, and the police who'd drawn the short straw of having to keep them apart, Donald is so flat that a piece of rising ground outside of town had the title *Mount* Jeffcott, which was only a slightly less likely mount than the forty-metre-high Mount Wycheproof half an hour's drive away.

Unlike Sally's home turf there were no ice rinks, cinemas, multi-storey shopping centres or art galleries, although there is an impressive agricultural museum in Donald. If four years in Ballarat, a city of sixty thousand people, and another year in Stawell on the flanks of the Grampians were an introduction to country life, this was another country. If she hadn't been teaching, homemaking, housekeeping and helping out the local netballers and constantly driving back and forth to Ballarat and Melbourne for Country Week matches, I don't know what she would have done with her spare time.

I settled into the lifestyle with a passion. I was incredibly social and involved in a whole range of activities, ambling along and pursuing whatever interested me. Teaching was only a minor hindrance to an otherwise full life. School gave me the structure I needed to get by, the school bells told me when I should be there, when I should eat and when I should go home, and then the school holidays came along, as they had since I was five years old, and gave me a break from the routine. I filled the rest of the week in as I liked, going to the pub or the races or barbecues at the football club. Family were important and they fitted in somewhere—just somewhere—and I lived a life of what I now call the line of best fit, and that's to say I did what I wanted when I wanted.

For a while I thought I'd done well, choosing a job I was getting by on without being particularly challenged while I had a ball out of hours. A physical education teacher's clothes were comfortable and wet hair for the first class of the day might indicate I'd been working out in the gym before school. So long as I turned up at school shortly before the students and outstayed them by a few minutes, all seemed well.

After a while the Education Department began sending me student-teachers to exploit: young people who did my work for me while I supposedly observed their performance and gave them feedback. There wasn't a lot to tell a lot of them as they were already better teachers than I was so I used my time more productively elsewhere.

One of those student-teachers, Gerard Murphy, had followed a similar path to mine, from a country town, in his case Minyip, to teachers' college at Ballarat. I think I saw a little bit of me in him. As it happened I was wrong because he was actually a reasonably responsible person. Such was Gerard's competence and enthusiasm for the job that it was probably during his placement that my doubts about my own performance peaked. Who ought to be supervising who?

Where there was latitude at school or home to skip on what I regarded as chores I left them to others while I got on with more important tasks. I had team-bonding sessions at the football club to attend, horses that had to be backed, sports telecasts that had to be watched. Looking back, I was a … anyway, let's move on.

~

WE WERE MARRIED IN 1984, four weeks before my father died. Life does go on because it must but never quite the same as it was. We stayed busy, rolling along largely as before with Sally taking care of our responsibilities while I stayed as physically and socially active—well, having as much fun—as I possibly could.

When we were married we agreed that if we had a child I would have the opportunity to have at least a year staying home and becoming what is now fashionably called a househusband.

Our first child, Courtney, was born three years later and when I'd finished celebrating my lynchpin role in bringing a child into the world I settled into another four or five months of teaching while Sally stayed at home. I can remember looking forward to a rest when it was my turn to stay at home with the new baby.

There weren't a lot of househusbands anywhere in the 1980s and particularly not around Donald and, whatever they were saying down the pub, I wanted to spend that time with Courtney.

I knew it would be fantastic experience, staying home looking after our daughter and managing the house and doing those little things Sally had been taking care of for so long.

Sally went back to teaching physical education at the beginning of 1988, in effect taking over my teaching allotment at the high school, and I stayed home, my only responsibilities our seven-month-old daughter and home duties.

I'd underestimated at a very practical level, perhaps, what parents who choose to stay at home go through. It was an enlightening experience in terms of how organised you had to be, how a child might not necessarily fit into the plans you had laid out and how difficult it was spending so much time, not on your own, but with someone who didn't talk back to you.

All of those were significant lessons, but for me it was an opportunity to do something I don't think I'd ever done effectively before and that was to think. I found myself thinking long and hard about what I wanted out of my work and what we were trying to achieve in life as a couple and, more importantly now, as a family. There was enormous self-reflection.

I realised I had many things to be thankful for, not the least a stable upbringing in what was a fairly sheltered and very happy home, Dad in a stable work doing a job he obviously loved and a mother who was willing to support us in every way she possibly could. But that raised all kinds of questions in my mind about our situation and how we'd go further down the track, and how I'd go providing for others a stable environment similar to the one I'd had provided for me.

The other recognition was how fortunate I was right then to be in the situation I was. After a relatively easy ride to adulthood and a secure career I was now being afforded the luxury of time to be able to think my situation through while Sally supported me emotionally and financially.

Until then my life goals could have been summarised as to have a good time and to live forever. Not that I hadn't been setting myself goals, I had. But they were usually physical challenges rather than lifestyle or career goals.

Typically, I'd started long-distance running with the aim of one day finishing a marathon. After that? Run another one. I began to recognise that I was dealing with the symptoms of restlessness rather than its causes. Nevertheless, I'd come to value the training runs as good thinking time so I kept at it, pounding the back roads around Donald contemplating ideas like, 'If you don't have goals yourself, you'll have to work for someone who does' and trying to make some practical sense of them.

Goals? For eight years I'd been enjoying teaching largely for the comforts, not goals. Meeting a challenge was finding someone who had one and giving them a hand with it. I'd arranged my life so I could continue soft-pedalling, avoid heavy lifting and stay well within my comfort zone. Now, where teaching is concerned it's not entirely true that you only get out of it what you put into it because I got something out of it. But I was a long, long way from the teacher I'd hoped and imagined I'd be when secondary school finished and teachers' college beckoned.

For the first time in my life I was wondering why I was doing what I was doing. And not just teaching. It was an across-the-board re-evaluation. So much of what I was doing was habit-based and I'd been rolling along as if it would go on forever.

It was fascinating to start thinking through those questions when, maybe for the first time, the answers actually mattered to me: Why did I do what I did back then? Why am I doing what I'm doing now? Am I happy teaching? Where do I really want to be and what do I want to be doing when my daughter has grown up?

How does a parent provide a stable, happy home when they don't like their work? Many parents manage it but I was far from convinced I could be one of them. And if a parent does eventually recognise they've a problem with their work and decide to do something about it, how easy is it to change careers without causing hardship for the entire family?

Asking the same questions of myself I always had, but projecting decades rather than months ahead, the answers were vastly different. Was I ready and willing to commit to another thirty years around secondary schools? It was becoming increasingly difficult to answer in the affirmative and there wasn't much time left to do something about it. But what?

~

THE HIGH SCHOOL was short of staff one day and I was asked if I'd like a break from home duties and come back as an emergency teacher. There was no doubt my dark attitudes had been affecting our home life and, I thought, if a day here and there of emergency teaching breaks up the routine and sparks me up a bit, it'd be a worthwhile exercise.

Returning to school after the time away, I looked at how it worked and how my colleagues functioned and I was taken aback by how negative and disillusioned I'd become. The emergency teaching had only served to make me more concerned about my situation. I had a feeling I was treading water, marking time, in the doldrums, not even going in circles. I went home to re-examine what I was doing and why I was doing it and to question, again, how well I'd been teaching.

Teaching, I thought, is such an important vocation. Parents trust their children to you at a vitally important time in the young person's development but there was a glaring incongruity between the value we all say we put on a good education and the reality of school as I knew it. Teachers must have some influence on the views and therefore the lives of their students and that, I was now thinking, carried much more responsibility than I thought it had during the eight years I'd been teaching. As a teacher I just went through the motions; turned up, taught and left. Schools and classrooms as I knew them were a place to do time in. I responded to the sound of the bell and the rest was a reflex response. Were the kids or my work colleagues getting as much value out of me as I felt they should?

There was a huge discrepancy between my current path and where I'd wanted to be down the track so there was a dissatisfaction and a lack of fulfilment with my situation but no idea of how to resolve it. I had a sense of wanting more autonomy over my working life, thinking that if I had more control over my work perhaps I'd feel differently about it. I decided that a change of school would not have been enough.

I knew I wouldn't just step off the cliff, so to speak. What were the ways I could use my degree without risking the family's financial security? I wanted to do something different, preferably something I could be passionate about, but above all else it had to pay a living wage from day one. At that particular point in time it still wasn't at all clear about what that might be but I started to explore some options.

The Tears of a Clown

In a program of action there are risks and costs but they are far less than the long-term costs of comfortable inactivity.
JOHN F. KENNEDY

JOB SECURITY HAS ITS OWN BURDENS and one of those is that it's essentially up to you to initiate a career change.

Teachers often talk among themselves about alternative careers and there were always plenty of stories floating about the staffroom about those who'd left the fold. Everyone had heard about the maths teacher who'd thrown it all in to become a deep-sea diver and salvaged a Spanish galleon full of gold coins. Or, alternatively, the librarian who became a professional punter and lost their superannuation in two weeks. And there was always a steady supply of farcical stories about teachers who'd joined the military.

So I'd known anecdotally for some years that there was a role in the defence forces for people with a teaching degree. But exactly what it was I had no idea. Do they get shot at? Do they teach soldiers or their kids? Humanities or ballistics? I decided I'd make enquiries to all three branches of the military and see what they had to say.

I called the army first. The person I spoke to said, 'Yes, you'd be teaching adults. You'd be a soldier first and then a teacher' and that I probably wouldn't get shot at. 'But you never know,' she said, laughing. That left two.

I rang the navy and their response was similar to the army's. They said you rarely get shot in the navy, only blown up or drowned.

To this day I don't know if the army and navy knew the air force were playing dirty pool with their recruiting pitch, but when I rang the RAAF recruitment office the person I spoke to said straight away, 'So how would you feel if you didn't teach again?' I didn't hear another word they said and got them to mail me an application form.

Not being entirely sure of what I wanted and not being entirely clear about what the RAAF education officer's role involved suited me; the lack of certainty was appetising after so long on a diet of predictability. I knew the air force wasn't my ultimate destination and, without knowing where it might lead, at least it would be somewhere different. And who could know what doors it might open?

This was very big news to Sally. We were both flat out playing with and coaching local sports teams and involved in all sorts of community activities and had another child on the way so, with no reason to think otherwise, Sally had been planning on us staying in our recently renovated old house and life going on much as it had at Donald, in a great school with terrific kids, committed staff and supportive parents. And why not? Sally hadn't heard anything to the contrary. How could I have gone so far down the track of contemplating a radical career change without properly communicating to Sally that I was dissatisfied with the teaching life? That self-centred oversight is as good an illustration as there is of my state of mind then, operating on auto-pilot and just assuming Sally would know how I'd been thinking.

~

I DROVE FROM DONALD TO THE RAAF base at Laverton, near Melbourne, and spoke to some former teachers and tried to get a sense of what their lives were. As I learned, education officers went through three months of officer training and then graduated to the School of Radio at the Laverton base, or to Wagga Wagga where most RAAF apprentices were trained.

What struck me most from talking with them was their description of officer training and how physically rigorous it had been. Being physically tested for three months and facing leadership and teamwork challenges held some attraction for me and the regimentation wasn't an issue so long as it was different to what I'd known.

Joining the air force would be breaking the mould I'd been growing into for nearly three decades. I'd been around schools as a toddler, had seven years of primary school, six years of secondary school, four years of university and then eight years of teaching. How would I go outside the school gates?

I went back to Donald. Sally was still teaching and I was still at home looking after Courtney so I had some valuable thinking time. Would I return to secondary teaching in 1989 or, perhaps, join the RAAF and for really the first time in my life, head into uncharted territory. It was a big decision, joining the air force, but returning to secondary teaching would in many ways have been an even bigger one. If I wasn't sure about the air force I knew I wouldn't go back to secondary teaching so, in that sense, the air force became the softer option.

Filling out the RAAF application form, it felt like I'd been raised in captivity. I'd lived in Education Department premises, been educated in Education Department-administered schools, trained to be a teacher in Education Department-sanctioned programs, and been on the Education Department payroll for all my working life. Here I was, nearly thirty years old, and making my first real job application.

For reasons I still don't quite understand—ignorance, naïve self-confidence or having lived too sheltered an existence, perhaps—I was largely oblivious to the selection criteria, the purpose of the pre-selection interviews or the fact that the RAAF do actually knock people back. Yet I had an overwhelming and completely unjustified belief throughout the application process that I'd be accepted. Looking back on it I cringe at my utter lack of knowledge about what I was getting myself into and how I approached the interviews.

After a series of visits to the recruiting centre in St Kilda Road, I received a letter in August 1989 offering me officer training at RAAF Williams, the airbase west of Melbourne at Point Cook. But there were some major hurdles.

I would have to live on the airbase for the three months of officer training and contact with families was limited. Seeing Sally every second weekend would be difficult if not impossible, and

I'd become extremely attached to Courtney and our newly arrived son, Jackson, and I seriously doubted that I'd be able to cope without day-to-day contact with them. Sally would have to manage on her own with a two-year-old and a young baby. Plus, when officer training finished and we were reunited as a family, we would be posted to wherever the RAAF saw fit.

~

THE WESTGATE BRIDGE is no place to be driving behind a curtain of tears but that's when it hit me, on our way to Point Cook, that there was no going back now on joining the RAAF, nor, short of the unthinkable and I was drummed out of there as a dud round, would I be returning to Donald High School. If the military accepted notes like schools do I would have got Sally to write one there and then; 'Dear Air Force, Ray can't attend today as he's got a stomach upset.'

We—myself, Sally, Courtney and the four-month-old Jackson—kept on going anyway, Jackson and I bawling away like the Two Tenors as we drove through the new housing develop-ments and down the narrow road through farmland that leads to the airbase. Through a blur of tears and beyond the candy-striped boom gates I could see the military-looking buildings in neat lines, the hallowed dirt of the parade ground, arrays of flagpoles, some sports fields, and kilometres of concrete runway surrounded by hectares of tarmac and massive hangars and dilapidated outbuildings where aircrew trained for the Battle of Britain. There was a large military aviation museum crammed with wire-and-canvas biplanes, Second World War fighters, gigantic cargo planes and a Vietnam-era F-4 Phantom. There were pilots in g-suits inspecting aircraft before heading off to practice formation aerobatics at a thousand kilometres an hour and stark reminders everywhere that military aviation is a very, very serious business. But, I remember thinking, not half as serious as leaving your family and Donald behind for three months. I wept uncontrollably for the next hour or so.

Eventually it was made pretty clear that the family couldn't stay for the duration of officer training and they would have to leave. As they headed off, I wondered—and I bet Sally was wondering, too—how I'd make it through the night, let alone three months. How would I have gone in wartime? 'Dear Mr Churchill, Ray can't attend bombing over Europe today because he can't stop crying.'

When you enter officer training you train with people from different backgrounds who'd been admitted by direct entry as I had, and also those who were promoted to be an officer from the ranks of the RAAF. Some people on the course had no real connection with the military or any kind of military upbringing and like me were learning from scratch, while the seasoned airmen and airwomen had a very clear understanding of the military culture and all its ramifications. Me? I was from Donald.

On my first night on base we were standing at the bar getting to know one another and I vividly recall asking one of my new colleagues which team he barracked for and he said 'Penrith Panthers.' I said, 'No, in Australian football,' and he said, 'Who cares?' My work was going to change, the culture was different and my past, the thing I'd traded on for the best part of thirty years, counted for nil. The dehumanising haircut was a breeze after that.

That's when the implications of what I'd chosen to do really started to hit home. To all intents and purposes any risk in terms of relationships and career had been insignificant up to that point. Without my past dictating the present, who was I now? What would I be in the future without a school to hang my hat on? How would I go for three months in a social vacuum, with none of the personal and cultural touchstones to remind me who I was? Would I be the same person? If RAAF training changed me, what would change? Would my family know me? Would I know me? Did I really want to change everything? Or only a few things? Dissatisfaction with who I was and where I was going had initiated a chain of events that led to me sitting on the end of a single bunk in a dormitory, wondering how unhappy I'd actually been previously. If I was goose-fart unhappy then, I was thunderclap unhappy now. What had I done? I'd joined the air force seeking security and more than anything I'd ever done previously, this was risking *everything*. I'd seen myself previously as being largely a product of the Education Department and now I was handing myself over to another institution. If I didn't get shot, what kind of product would I turn out to be this time?

As I learned down the track, one of the fundamentals of leadership is to know yourself and be comfortable with who you are. I was a long, long way short of that when I joined the RAAF.

~

IT WAS A HARD ROAD. The bulk of my course was made up of younger men than me who after officer training would go on to East Sale to be trained as aircrew and progress from there to being navigators.

The typical day meant being up and ready to get underway with physical training at 5.30 a.m., followed by classes throughout the day, some of them practical, some in the classroom. There was more physical training in the late afternoon, with barely enough of the day remaining for washing and ironing and polishing and a lot of other things I wasn't very good at that took me forever.

What stood out early on was my inability to accept the military discipline. At school we'd always encouraged questions and discussion so I thought it a good idea to ask a lot of questions to show them I was interested. That was a mistake.

The hardest part to accept early on was how the entire group suffered the consequences of my screwing up. And not just because I asked too many questions. If I'd not made the bed properly or folded the shirts the right way, everyone had to do it all over again. I did eventually learn that in the military you just have to shut your mouth and do exactly as you are told. But it took a while

Luckily I was surrounded by people who did know what was going on and why, and went out of their way to coach me. One in particular, Kraig Grime, had come from the ranks into officer training and recognised immediately that I didn't have a clue and had the potential to make his three months of leadership training a living nightmare. I heard afterwards that he'd asked an instructor if he'd pass the course if he buried me in a shallow grave near the end of the runway and they said no, he'd still have to be assessed on merit. With so few other options available to him, Kraig showed me how to make a bed so a coin bounced on it, how to shave properly and check that my belt was through every loop.

There was a rigid routine but we were expected to be responsive so there was always the possibility we'd be called out without notice on an exercise in the bush. Having your pack ready to go was essential because periodically we'd be woken at three or four o'clock in the morning, put on the back of trucks and sent off into the darkness to a surprise destination.

We might find ourselves in the You Yangs or the Grampians, or maybe the Wombat State Forest, locations I knew courtesy of being a lifelong Victorian. So if the idea of being sound asleep one moment and a couple of minutes later blasting down the highway in the back of a truck was unsettling, it probably wasn't quite as disturbing to someone like me with local knowledge as it might have been for someone who'd, say, come down from tropical Queensland a couple of weeks earlier and had no idea where we were heading and what might be at the end of the road.

To have found the grit to get through something that wasn't quite as I'd imagined it was worthwhile and I learned a lot about decision-making, hardship, and developing camaraderie within the group. But too often I struggled to make sense of how we were training.

There were some incredibly positive lessons in it but some aspects seemed, well, mindless. Often the only lesson I could see was learning how to show blind obedience, which seemed to me to be the antithesis of leadership and more of a threat to good teamwork than a basis for it. Not that I knew for sure, but that's how it looked and that's how I felt.

I spent hour after hour marathon training on the roads around Point Cook and kept my mind busy trying to sort through what I thought had been useful leadership training and what hadn't. I combed through it and combed through it again to see if I'd missed anything and found myself at odds with some aspects of the training we were receiving. I was asking the questions I'd been asking as a secondary student. What were we meant to be learning? Why are we learning it this way?

I'd slowly learned not to upset the instructors by asking probing questions in class and left it to times where more amenable responses were likely and the impression I often got was that it was the first time in living memory anyone had asked. I was surprised by the 'I don't know but that's the way we've always done it' responses—they weren't far removed from some of the thinking, or lack of it, I'd encountered in schools.

The training was extremely effective—there was no doubt about that—and the Point Cook training programs were clearly some of the best ever devised anywhere for any purpose because the results were on the board. There was also a widespread belief that, because no stone had been left unturned, the training couldn't be improved. But I was finding plenty of unturned stones and that suggested to me that perhaps the training could be improved, although I had no idea how.

At times during officer training I wondered whether I would in fact renege on my obligation and go back home to Donald to resume teaching and try and pick up life as it was. But as the weeks passed, I became a little more resilient and the hardships seemed not quite so hard as they had before. Until then, I think, given the stability of my life, I'd been very much a fair-weather traveller and I was finding some skills I hadn't known I had. I'd taken a few risks and I was still here and that was a significant lesson to me.

The philosophies underlying the leadership training had me intrigued and I was beginning to think, for the first time in my life, that there was a particular area of work that really interested me. I kept on pounding the roads around Point Cook building up to a marathon and arguing with myself about the pros and cons about the training we were receiving. Hundreds of hours and thousands of kilometres of later, I was forming some strong opinions of my own about leadership and teamwork training that were, alas, contrary to many of the ways the military worked. So as gratified as I was to graduate from officer training, I certainly wasn't thinking of the RAAF as a long-term career.

November 1990 was notable for a couple of achievements; I ran non-stop all the way from Frankston to Melbourne and, as I crossed the finish line another runner congratulated me on finishing my first marathon. It was better than that, I said, 'I got two marathons in one—my first and last.'

~

As the end of officer training approached, thoughts turned to our likely postings. Most of the course attendees came from northern Australia and wanted postings to Amberley in Queensland or Williamstown at Newcastle—anywhere north of Point Cook. Wherever we'd be sent and by whatever mysterious process, it was out of our hands. We'd hear at the last moment, bid one another farewell and go. It was a major distraction.

A padre on our course had some fun with me, saying, 'I've remembered you in my prayers, Ray, and you will be posted to Point Cook,' which was a brave call given the odds of that happening were close to zero. Education officers' first posting was almost invariably to a training base, either Laverton or Wagga.

When I was eventually assigned to Occupational Analysis at the newly established Training Command at RAAF Williams, Point Cook, the padre was more surprised than I was—I just figured he'd had some inside information—and after that an increasing number of people sought his opinions on racehorses, football teams and anything else that might make some money.

My new job at Training Command was, put very simply, reviewing training. We travelled from base to base, consulting senior tradesmen and conducting elaborate surveys and then using the results to modify the apprentice training. Aside from being based in Victoria, the biggest advantage was that I got to see most of the RAAF training facilities very early on and got an overview of the various roles education officers played.

The reality for any organisation operating aircraft is that flyers are, numbers-wise, only a small part of the equation. The aircrew are 'the sharp end', the tip of an organisational iceberg made up largely of 'blunts' like me or anyone else who wasn't aircrew.

The idea of working with Sharps appealed to me. Given the demanding and unforgiving nature of their work, I was far more interested in delivering that kind of training than, say, working as a librarian or teaching radio call-signs by rote. Aviation, and military aviation in particular, has been forensically examined for decades in the quest for safer planes and pilots and, I thought, if there was one area I'd be exposed to highly evolved training programs, it would be among the aviators. But such was the ratio of Blunts to Sharps, most training was conducted by Blunts for Blunts and the specialist nature of the Sharps work meant you had to be pretty sharp to teach them much at all. I'd only ever flown up the back of Airbuses.

At RAAF Edinburgh, an airbase about thirty kilometres north of Adelaide, I came across a small training unit known as the Airmen Aircrew Flying Training School. AAFTS had as part of its responsibilities managing leadership and teamwork training for the Maritime Patrol Group, which maintained and operated the RAAF's fleet of Lockheed P-3 Orions that flew coastal surveillance and long-range search-and-rescue missions. The MPG had a unique reputation within the air force for seeing themselves as teams that had to function incredibly well and for having team structures that largely defied rank.

I kept in touch with the education officer who was at AAFTS and when he said he might be moving to Wagga Wagga I contacted the Canberra office that looked after postings and indicated my interest if the position became available at Edinburgh. It did in early 1991 and three weeks or so after our third child, Jesse, was born, we moved to Adelaide.

It was a fascinating environment to be working in. The Maritime Patrol Group are elite performers by any standard. With a history that stretched back fifty years to Catalina flying boats the squadron's work has always been essentially the same—nerve-wracking flights over massive stretches of ocean—and with so little margin for error that failures of teamwork can be disastrous.

~

WHEN I ARRIVED AT THE Airmen Aircrew Flying Training School, asking myself the usual questions about what was being learned and why it was being learned the way it was, I was surprised by how readily it was accepted that what the school did now was done largely because it had always been done that way. Yet a lot of the training had, as far as I could see, no particular learning objective. For example, there was a regular session, the morning brief, when students had to stand before the group with officers and instructors in the room while they were assaulted with problems that required mental arithmetic or reciting complicated procedures. The marks were recorded and made public and there were penalties for wrong answers.

Even as an instructor who didn't have to answer the questions I found the environment frightening. The students, I imagine, must have entered that room petrified and stayed that way for the duration of the session. It continued a tradition that went back decades but I couldn't see how the students or the RAAF gained anything from it. How did it help make them better students? How did it make them better airmen when they returned to the squadron to do their jobs? I knew that for theory-based subjects time had to be spent just sitting down in a classroom learning about the mechanics or the technical side of their craft. But we were employing similar theoretical techniques to teach practical skills like leadership and teamwork, the underlying presumption apparently being that if you knew it you could do it. I doubted that.

As I'd learned at Point Cook, questioning the training's value was rarely welcomed and I eventually learned to ask questions in a way that wasn't going to alienate the instructors I had to work with. Most of the instructors, given the right approach, were prepared to listen to queries and were open to suggestions that changes in methodology or process might actually improve the quality of the training and turn out a better product.

I was very fortunate in that shortly after I arrived at the unit the commanding officer, who held a similar view to mine about the worth of a theoretical approach to practical skills, gave me the licence to start looking into revamping our leadership training. The CO was incredibly supportive, giving me enough scope to act and frequently saying to me that by 'revamp' he didn't mean adjusting or rewriting the training packages. He wanted the leadership and teamwork training re-evaluated from scratch.

~

I'D HEARD AN EX-RAAF OFFICER, Peter O'Brien, refer to air force training as having two components, mechanics and dynamics, and when I arrived at AAFTS the emphasis was firmly on the mechanics. Learning was meant to result from long lectures, overhead transparencies and bored students. Examinations confirmed a student could repeat information by rote and it was assumed that this knowledge would translate into the set of practical skills required for effective leadership. There was no evidence that it did, just an assumption that it would.

For the leadership training, perhaps a week-long exercise in the bush, each student led the others through a navigation exercise that might require the leader to show initiative at various points along the way. But, in the end, it was reduced to a box-ticking exercise. Had the student briefed the group effectively? Had they delegated effectively? Did they lead effectively? And we'd go through a checklist and pass or fail the student, based on our opinion as observers.

When I first saw that assessment framework in action it highlighted to me the difference of opinion I'd had with all the leadership training I'd seen and that was that the lack of attention paid to the followers' opinions of their leaders' performances. Surely the followers' opinions of the leadership they'd received were at least as important as anyone else's. And more informative, I would have thought, than the views of an observer. But we didn't engage the students in any peer evaluation and that seemed flawed to me.

I realised at that stage that I wasn't equipped to handle the more experiential types of learning I was advocating. I would have to break out of what I now call teaching mode into facilitator mode so I could elicit information from the group to enhance the learning process without igniting a brawl and to do this I would need some new skills of my own.

Wearing Some Feedback

*Honest criticism is hard to take, particularly from
a relative, friend, acquaintance, or stranger.*
FRANKLIN P. JONES

WHILE TRYING TO REDESIGN the leadership course at the Airmen
Aircrew Flying Training School to favour experiential learning
ahead of theory, the RAAF was developing its Airmen Education
and Training Scheme that was also using an experiential
methodology.

To equip me to conduct experiential training, I was sent on a
two-week facilitators' course at Wagga Wagga run by a private
consulting group. I went into it believing I knew most of what I
needed to know, and as the course unfolded I found out that I was
a long way short of the mark.

The facilitator was exceptional, encouraging self-analysis and
taking us through an exercise that emphasised how counter-
productive—and prevalent—value judgments could be in the
team-building process. We learned how to frame questions and
statements in a non-judgmental fashion and how to set up an
environment where the participants were less fearful of giving
honest, useful feedback and receiving it in turn.

It was a soul-searching fortnight for me, with intensive peer evaluation after nearly every exercise. We were constantly rating one another's performances and were expected to be open and honest with one another every step of the way, knowing that at the end of the course we'd be selecting from those among us who we considered to be the best candidates for leadership positions within the Airmen Education and Training Scheme.

People are naturally reluctant to hear their peers' assessment of their performance, no matter what team or working environment they are in. But this course had been set up to push us right to the edge in that area and whether we initially liked the idea or not, we grew so accustomed to giving and receiving feedback that very quickly we came to expect it.

I recall sitting in a circle after one exercise and receiving some acerbic feedback about my performance as a facilitator and thinking that it was the some of the frankest—and most useful—advice I'd ever received. In the midst of that session I realised that, maybe for the first time in my life, I wasn't in fear of giving or receiving feedback and was actually beginning to welcome those opportunities. Once we'd become comfortable with the concept as a group and realised the feedback was the key to our improvement, I think we all looked forward to the feedback sessions.

I was deeply impressed by the environment the facilitator had created, where honest feedback was delivered and received dispassionately and without any other agenda but to improve one another's performances.

That process of doing a group exercise followed by a facilitated peer evaluation and feedback session was as powerful a learning experience as I'd ever been exposed to and it confirmed in my mind that experiential learning was probably the best way for our students at the AAFTS to learn practical leadership skills.

~

I HADN'T QUITE UNDERSTOOD the changes that I'd undergone on the course until some time afterwards. A number of people at work said that I seemed different and Sally said I was operating differently at home. I was listening to people more than I had in the past and seemed more willing to accept other people's views rather than focusing on what I thought was right or wrong. I'd unequivocally learned on the course that different people can have entirely different takes on a particular situation and whether an opinion was valid or invalid was far less important than exploring and trying to understand why the person thought that way.

Those kind of facilitation skills would, I thought, be incredibly useful in leadership training at the AAFTS. But there was a major obstacle to obtaining honest feedback in the air force environment—the students' fear of failing the leadership training component. That was perfectly natural given that a failure saw them removed from the course and detrimentally affected their careers thereafter.

We had to find a way to alleviate that fear so the AAFTS students could be honest about one another's performance during leadership training and the only way that was going to happen was if the students were secure in the knowledge that their taking issue with the way something had been done wasn't sabotaging a colleague's career.

So, before going out with one group on a week-long leadership assessment exercise in the bush, I called the students in and said I would guarantee each of them a pass so long as I believed they were being honest about one another's performances as leaders.

Unlike the previous box-ticking assessments of leadership abilities we'd been using at AAFTS, this time we sat in a circle and openly and honestly evaluated how the leader had performed in communicating what was to be done and how the tasks had been allocated.

One student had driven a group mercilessly. In his mind he'd done what was required of him because he'd completed the task on time. And using the traditional assessment guidelines he most certainly would have passed because the task was completed on time so the boxes would have been ticked off and that would have been the end of it.

But when we sat down afterwards to look at how he might improve his performance as a leader he received some very strident feedback from the group, who in reality were using a far more comprehensive set of performance criteria than any checklist we'd ever devised. Their feedback suggested that his leadership style was in fact deeply flawed; he'd given no thought whatsoever to how efficiently the group had performed the task, how fatigued they were by the end of it or how that would have affected their capacity for work the following day. As obvious as his shortcomings were once they'd been raised, they certainly weren't obvious until someone actually raised them.

In my role as an observer I couldn't know for sure how the task had affected them physically and morale-wise. Nor, without the feedback session, would any of the students have known that they were unanimous in their condemnation of the leader's approach. There was nothing on the checklists AAFTS had been using for decades to account for a task being satisfactorily completed despite unsatisfactory leadership.

The ramifications of the peer evaluation sessions were, I thought, profound. Of the thousands of RAAF aircrew who'd graduated from leadership training over the past sixty or seventy years, I wondered, how many had done so when their peers had thought of them as lousy leaders?

~

As I WAS TRYING TO CHANGE the content of the AAFTS's practical subjects like leadership training, I was also trying to change the style of instruction from teaching to facilitating and using experiential learning. The basic method was to do a task and then learn from it by afterwards looking at it from a perspective of what worked, what didn't, and how it might be done better next time. The idea was to give students the information they needed to modify their behaviour and then the opportunity to put it into practice and become, in this case, better leaders. I tabled the ideas for discussion because the different style of instruction had implications for the other instructors.

From an instructor's point of view, the lecture is a safe option. There's little if any engagement with the students; you walk in, open the folders, put on the overhead transparencies, the students take notes, you deliver some premeditated words and you leave. The students sit an examination which is supposedly some kind of gauge of the instructor's ability to engage the students in learning. But the exam doesn't prove anything, of course, because students go away and study hard just before the exam and it's never entirely clear what's been genuinely learned and what's a short-term memory from the previous night's study session that is forgotten the moment the exam is over.

I've heard a lecture defined as 'a method of getting notes from the pad of the teacher to the pad of the student without the information passing through the brain of either'. I thought that described pretty well a lot of what we'd been doing at the AAFTS.

One of my roles at the school was to sit in with instructors and observe them in action and give them feedback that might encourage them to advance their skills.

In one memorable session I watched an instructor begin a lecture standing next to the overhead projector and stay there for the remainder of the session, slipping a new transparency under the projector every couple of minutes. Sure enough, not long into the session a student in the front row nodded off and started snoring. The instructor continued wading through the material, transparency after transparency, while the student dozed on, periodically gasping for air and then dropping off again.

At the end of, for want of a better description, 'the lesson', I asked the instructor how he felt the session had gone and he said,

'Yeah, it went well, we got through the material.' His measure of learning was the number of overhead transparencies he got through. I queried him about the student who was asleep and he said, 'Well, that was his choice.' It was a terrific example of the treadmill-type teaching mentality I'd seen too much of previously in schools and universities, and I decided there and then I would never again use or support that style of teaching because I was now convinced it had nothing whatsoever to do with learning.

~

IF I WAS SERIOUS ABOUT developing practical leadership training courses and facilitation skills for the instructors, I needed to find support and feedback about its liabilities. That is, I needed someone who could objectively assess whether what I was developing was in fact a sound learning model.

I was fortunate at the time to have been doing some joint project work with the base psychologist Joanne Hamilton. Like the rest of we Blunts, Joanne had struggled to gain access to the insular world of the aircrew.

While I delivered and facilitated the leadership program, Joanne came in, sometimes as a co-facilitator but more often as an observer of the experiential approach I was developing, and evaluated the exercises and the programs I was using in terms of the learning outcomes for the students and the product—that is, students with a capacity for showing initiative and leadership— that we were sending back to the squadrons. Joanne's role expanded as we started to look at a team development program some of the aircrews were embarking on.

When aircrew arrived at the squadron they were allocated their position in a particular crew. A crew consisted of two pilots, two flight engineers, a tactician, a navigator, a sensor manager and up to six electronics analysts.

There was extraordinary attention to detail in aviators' technical training and every box had to be ticked off, but then, when the crews were put together, they performed differently. And that's when we started to question the dynamics side of the teamwork equation. Recalling Peter O'Brien's observation, that there are the mechanics and the dynamics of team—or, as some others describe them, the physics and the chemistry—it was clear that the aircrew received rigorous technical training in relation to the mechanics of their jobs. But the dynamics were still largely a puzzle.

Joanne and I drafted up a prospective training course and fortunately the Commanding Officer of No 11 Squadron supported our pilot program.

The feedback we received from the first aircrew that did the training was extraordinarily positive, their responses unequivocally supporting my belief that experiential training combined with regular peer feedback and evaluation sessions amounted to a very powerful learning tool. Most significantly, the overwhelming majority of the training's recipients concluded, just as I had after I'd undergone the facilitators' training course at Wagga Wagga, that the process had fundamentally changed the way they looked at team dynamics.

As positive as the early results were, Joanne and I were committed to the idea that the program wasn't static and it should at the very least embody some of the principles we were devising for the aircrew, and not for any ideological reasons but because it had become patently clear to me that seeking out feedback on your performance was the best way to improve it. So we constantly sought feedback from aircrew, asking them as we went along what worked, what didn't, and how we could do better. As we took that feedback on board, the program evolved and became an increasingly effective learning experience for those undergoing the training.

I was beginning to think that, perhaps, the idea might have broader applications outside the RAAF. The MPG aircrews' work was highly specialised but the effective component of the training was far from it. For that we'd sat in a circle, more often than not on some grass in the shade of some gum trees, and talked about what had happened earlier and how it might be done better next time. Far from being hi-tech, it was verging on no-tech. If the lessons learned out in the bush were translating into improved team performances out over the Southern Ocean thousands of kilometres away from land, then why wouldn't they apply elsewhere? The training wasn't about aircraft, it was about people working together and improving their performance irrespective of the actual work involved.

To define a group's common goals from the outset of the training we were beginning to put to the aircrews questions like, 'How is your team or crew viewed by others?', 'How do you want your team to be viewed by others?', and then discussing within the group what sorts of behaviours the team needed to be displaying or eradicating to be that sort of team.

We put the aircrew through a series of exercises, either as a team of peers or with one of them in a leadership role, and they looked at their performances afterwards and compared them to how they wanted to be as a team or a crew. When a team locked onto a particular task they tended to behave as they always had, so if there were problems with communication or not listening to others, or someone who wouldn't allow others to have input into a task, the typical dysfunctional behaviours of poor teams would come to the surface. After the exercise had been completed, and with the goals the team had identified earlier as the points of reference, the team discussed which behaviours of its members were to be encouraged and which behaviours were seen as counter-productive. Within a very short time behaviours began to change—often after the first feedback and evaluation session— and the teams began to perform appreciably better.

The facilitator's role was to assist the participants to see how their individual behaviours affected their team's performance and to help them commit to making the changes required for the team to perform better, and that was a major test for me. Joanne Hamilton, as well as doing crucial work researching facilitation skills for reflective and experiential learning techniques and evaluating the program's learning outcomes, went out of her way to give me honest and sometimes fierce feedback on my performance as a facilitator. Joanne's work was invaluable then and remains so to this day and her impact on my skill development cannot be overstated.

While we were achieving terrific results with the aircrews I was beginning to realise that in such a large organisation with a hierarchy as rigid as the RAAF's, there were going to be some major difficulties in taking what we were doing beyond AAFTS and the squadrons. The Maritime Patrol Group's crews were unique, even within the RAAF, in that their sense of team almost defied rank; they were first and foremost team members because, I suspect, they knew only too well that if they were to return safely home they had to work well as a team. There was a heightened awareness among them that their fates were shared and if anything could be done improve the team's performance and, therefore, their odds of survival, then it was seen as being worthwhile.

I wasn't so sure about the rest of the air force though. No matter what the benefits were in terms of performance, the principles we'd devised would strike right at the foundations of traditional military structures and hierarchies. Being realistic, they weren't culturally compatible. Was the RAAF ready for a leadership framework where the rank and file counselled their superiors about changing their behaviour to improve the team's performance? Perhaps not.

That was a reality check of sorts because if the principles we'd developed had broader applications, I also had to acknowledge that some organisations were always going to opt for disciplined predictability over optimal team performance and would sooner rein in the team members' initiative than encourage it. But as we'd learned from the training we'd conducted, every team member has to show initiative because a lack of it seriously undermines effective leadership and teamwork.

Seeing the air force's traditional leadership training as institutionalising a culture of run-of-the-mill leadership and teamwork left me in an awkward position. If I was genuinely convinced — and I was — that the style of training we'd devised for AAFTS had advantages over the existing training methods in terms of learning outcomes and product — the leaders and teams it produced — then I was necessarily at odds with the leadership culture the RAAF had been developing for about eighty years.

While I'd met quite a few people in the air force who were open to constructive suggestion it wasn't like the place was knee deep in them and even if our training program was as valuable and effective as I believed it was, I could also imagine how its underlying principles would cause serious consternation among the people who actually ran the air force, many of whom had graduated with flying colours from the old school of leadership training.

I hadn't been looking at the RAAF as long-term career and there was always going to be a time when the military and I were going to part company and it was beginning to look as if it would be sooner rather than later. A couple of events brought that parting on much more quickly than even I had thought possible.

The routine of the air force and lack of control over posting cycles felt to me like the complete opposite of the autonomy I'd had in mind as a long-term goal when I left teaching. A new posting would inevitably happen but when and to where was out of our hands and for me as an education officer, a new posting invariably meant being assigned to a new role. That was likely to have been either as a librarian or back at a training school reviewing the syllabus or instructors' guides.

Having been among the Sharps for a couple of years doing by far the most interesting and rewarding work I'd ever done, I was particularly unenthusiastic, even rancorous, about the prospect of returning to what I felt was going to be a comparatively humdrum existence. I'd had strong doubts about leaving teaching to join the air force but they were molehills next to the mountains of doubt I had about slamming the lid shut on what we'd learned at AAFTS about teams and going quietly back to classrooms where the challenge was keeping the students awake. I didn't want to just walk away and in some ways felt I shouldn't just walk away as it looked like we might have stumbled on something worth persevering with. I'd been poring through books on the broader topic of leadership and teamwork—and there are hundreds of them—and none I saw seemed to have found the handle on team dynamics that we'd grabbed onto almost by accident, and it wasn't mired in obscure language or unfathomable mathematical concepts about standard deviations.

The underpinning principles weren't even patentable, they were too simple: Take any given team, find out what kind of team it really wants to be, give them some work to do and then afterwards help them talk honestly in their own language about how one another's behaviour matched up with that team they said they wanted to be; repeat the process, each time trying to do a little better than the last.

That's it. And there is only ever one result—individual and team performances improve.

A Whole New Ball Game

THE FRAMEWORK WOULD HAVE to be successfully tested in a different team environment to prove its soundness. I'd always seen the Sharps in the same light as elite sportspeople and perhaps it was that perception, combined with my physical education background and interest in sport, that had me wondering about how our model would apply to competitive team sports and, in particular, the sport I was most familiar with, Australian football.

In 1991 an air force colleague, Russell Evans, introduced me to Alan Stewart. Alan was midway through his first year as coach of Central District football club in the South Australian National Football League. Central District's home ground is just down the road from the airbase in Elizabeth.

Central District was like any other football club in that its clubrooms were decked out in inspirational messages about commitment and dedication. But they carried more than their fair share of irony given that Centrals were indisputably the least successful club in the SANFL at that stage, having never played a grand final since joining the league in 1964 or winning a final of any description since the early 1970s, and spending the vast majority of its thirty-year history anchored around the lower reaches of the ladder. The club had produced some wonderful footballers over the years—names like John Duckworth, Peter Jonas, John Platten and Gilbert McAdam—but team success wasn't the club's strong suit.

Alan had played for Central District in the late 1960s and early seventies, mainly in the reserves, and then become a decorated junior coach, taking the club's Under-17 team to two premierships in the late-1970s and then successfully coaching for a number of years South Australia's Teal Cup team—which we now call the Under-18 National Championships—before he took over the senior coaching role at Centrals at the beginning of 1991.

Alan's assistant coach was another club stalwart, Peter Jonas, and there was no doubt both of them had the club's long-term interests at heart. They made it clear they weren't interested in gimmicky quick-fix solutions, some of which the club had tried previously and nothing had changed.

Peter was Central's Under-17s best-and-fairest in the mid-70s, played in the Central's senior side shortly afterwards, and soon after that represented South Australia. In 1979 at the age of nineteen he was named in the All-Australian team and in 1981 headed off to North Melbourne in the VFL where he managed over the next six or seven years to rupture, tear or strain dozens of muscles and ligaments, break a couple of legs, a collarbone and a hand. In 1988, after eighty or so VFL games he returned to Centrals for another nineteen games and a broken arm.

Working closely with Alan and Peter Jonas was Peter Vivian, the club's reserves coach, who had played over three hundred games for Central District and again, was someone who desperately wanted to see the club succeed.

The 1992 season ended with Centrals finishing eighth in a nine-team competition. Alan decided that if he was going to be successful in his role as a senior coach he needed to take a longer and broader view than just coaching the team and that he'd somehow have to address a culture that had learned to survive on a steady diet of failure. He knew the club's history inside out and was determined to avoid what had happened in the past when the club had supposedly turned over a new leaf only to find not too far down the track that nothing had actually changed. He felt the club needed some kind of statement of values to give it a clear direction about where it wanted to go and some kind of structure to effect change and make it permanent, but without any clear idea of what kind of structure that might be.

We had a number of discussions about the leadership and teamwork principles we were developing within the air force and how they might be useful to the football club. There were obviously some drastic differences between the aviators and the footballers in terms of the work they do and the culture they do it in but, I said, if the principles we'd devised with the aircrews to optimise leadership and teamwork were universal, applying them to a struggling football club would have a number of consequences and improved on-field performances might well be one of them.

As we'd learned from the Maritime Patrol Group aircrew at the AAFTS, a particular set of conditions needed to be in place if teams were to work as effectively as they possibly could. The aircrew had unequivocally proven that where team performance is critical, then the best possible leadership and teamwork framework was very different to the 'star system' we're so familiar with. When near enough is nowhere near good enough and the job has to be done right, the so-called 'organisational pyramid' goes out the window and a whole new set of principles come into play. But those conditions tended to fly in the face of hierarchies and structures everyone from the military to business and government and sports clubs had traditionally used to organise themselves. And, as I'd learned, some organisations will happily sacrifice a team's performance rather than relinquish their control over it. Would a football club be any different?

The aircrew and footballers played for vastly different stakes but I'd not seen or read anything that said that optimal teamwork was only ever appropriate for life-and-death situations. Footballers do all sorts of training trying to improve the team's performance but they were largely exercises in the mechanics of the game. The dynamics were supposedly looked after by the coaches and beer.

For aircrews, the goals were relatively clear: complete the mission and land intact time and time again. A football team would first have to agree on what it regarded to be a successful mission. If the team decided its primary goal was to run around a bit and have a good time off the field, then Central District was already a howling success and my work was done. But if there were other goals, then as we'd done with the aircrews, we could explore how particular decisions impacted on the team achieving its objectives and see what they could learn from that. We could try introducing the leadership and teamwork principles applied by the aircrews—self-management, peer feedback and performance evaluation sessions and open lines of communication between all ranks—and see what happened. It would be a radical departure for an Australian football team or, for that matter, any sports team.

The risks were enormous for Alan and the two Peters, the club and, to a much lesser extent, myself. If the club hadn't been down so low and for so long I doubt anyone would have thought such radical pioneering surgery as being worth the risk.

It was going to be a high-wire act without a net but in the complete absence of anything resembling success that our opponents could point to, it'd be easier arguing for doing things differently. But there's ultimately only one measure by which the SANFL clubs measure themselves and that's winning football matches, and how long it would take before the framework helped improve the areas of the club's performance that won football matches was an open question. It'd be some kind of achievement if the framework helped the club discover it had all sorts of latent abilities but if they didn't eventually translate into winning more football matches then we'd have wasted everyone's time and probably our reputations.

We knew one thing. Winning more matches wouldn't happen immediately—it might not happen at all—and in the meantime there would be a lot of noses put out of joint by the process so we'd be working under a stopwatch and a microscope. I figured we'd have perhaps a season—twenty or so matches, or forty hours of football—to, if not completely turn around a thirty-year history of habitual underachievement, then at least show the club some dividends and release some of the internal pressures that would inevitably build up about the whacky new teambuilding ideas having wrecked the club's winning ways. With so little time on our hands, we'd have to get underway as soon as possible lest we'd end up as the latest entries on the long list of names that had sponsored change at a football club and comprehensively failed to improve the situation.

If the framework operated properly, individual footballer's behaviour would change for the benefit of the team. Before too long the club would learn to expect success in much the same way it had previously learned to expect failure, with the reasons behind that expectation of success no more obvious than the reasons behind its current expectations of failure.

Central District would have to learn to behave like a good team and see what happened after that. I thought the first step in that process was getting the players together and finding out how they saw themselves as a team now and comparing that with how they wanted to be seen. Once we'd identified where the team wanted to go, we'd look at how they'd need to behave to get there, and then help them work out a set of what in those days we called values but what I would now call core or 'trademark' behaviours. If we could work out what the team's 'trademarks' were going to be, we could work our way backwards into the kind of decision-making framework the club needed if it was going to be kind of club it wanted to be.

BONDING

Habits are the best of servants or the worst of masters.
NATHANIEL EMMONS

AT THE END OF 1992, AS ALAN STEWART entered his third year at Central District, I was invited to run the club's pre-season training camp. The camps have been a tradition around football clubs since John Kennedy and Tom Hafey built formidable VFL sides in the 1960s after putting their players through punishing physical fitness regimes in the off-season under athlete development legends like Percy Cerutty, Harry Gallagher and Franz Stampfl.

The camps are invariably held at the height of summer, a good opportunity to toughen the players up in the heat and for 'team bonding' with barbecues and beer in the work-hard-play-hard spirit I knew well from my time as a player. It'd been long understood, at least as long as I could remember, that football teams require an enormous amount of bonding if they're to be effective units as the alcohol breaks down social barriers and plays a crucial role in building esprit de corps. Or so the story goes.

As many footy club legends have been made on pre-season camps and post-season trips as on the field and if there's occasionally been serious repercussions from boys being boys, clubs have generally regarded the risks as worth it. As they say about footballers, money and the jumper don't matter because in the end they'll only go in for their mates. No stone has been left unturned or esky left unemptied in football's quest for a well-bonded team.

The lead up to the Central District pre-season camp was fascinating. The plan was for myself and Russell, assisted by John Miles, to run the weekend-long camp along experiential lines, doing exercises, then reflecting on the exercises and then relating the lessons back to their football. We met at the football club with Alan and the club's key off-field personnel so I could brief them about the camp and deal with any concerns or queries they might have had.

We would be camping out at Palmer, a rough piece of country in the Adelaide Hills. We'd mapped out some physically and mentally challenging team exercises and explained how they would work, and the logistics of the camp in terms of food and transport. It all went very smoothly and everyone there seemed happy with the plan as I'd explained it.

As I was about to leave Alan stopped me and asked me a question that in retrospect has probably had more impact on my understanding of the work I do and how I do it than any other question I've ever been asked.

Alan said, 'Ray, there's just one thing. What's your attitude about players drinking alcohol on the camp?'

Without thinking too hard, I said 'Is it a problem at your club?'

'Yes, it is.' There were nods of agreement from others around the table.

'Well,' I said, 'if that's the case, we might need to take as much alcohol out there as we can get our hands on and see what the players do.'

The table erupted. The comments all had a similar theme typified by the physical conditioning coach's view: 'We can't be taking grog out with these idiots. Who knows what they'll do?'

We debated the pros and the cons. I said I thought they were doing what many football clubs do, and that is to try and make rules to handle the problem. I argued that there'd be very little chance that Central District, or any other club for that matter, would improve if it believed people's behaviour could be improved by simply setting rules since a rule's power is only equal to the group's capacity to own the rule. No drinking after Thursday night, or no drinking through the week, or whatever the rule might be, is meaningless if the players don't own it because it won't change anything. If we told the players, 'Right, there'll be no alcohol on the camp,' they'd probably live with it for the weekend. Maybe some would try to sneak some in or some others might try to sneak out to get some. Who knows? But that wasn't going to get them to address alcohol as being an issue around their performance. We could pretend some rules had dealt with the problem, then go out and run up and down hills and around trees and over obstacles and sit down afterwards and talk about all the other things that in theory would improve their football.

Or, I argued, rather than tackling the problem the way so many football clubs and sporting teams do by setting rules, we could treat the entire weekend as an experiential learning situation and use it to try to get the players to understand the impact of their behaviour on their performance and take responsibility for it.

We eventually agreed that there would be alcohol on the camp, which was a relief given how hot and dusty it was going to be out there. On the way up to Palmer, Charlie the ultra-reliable team manager filled his car with more than enough beer to be sure we wouldn't run out before we'd learned anything worthwhile.

~

I WAS AT THE BOTTOM OF A GULLY when the players ambled into the camp along a dusty track and they looked to me a little bit like lambs on the way to their slaughter, entirely unaware of the physically demanding nature of the camp and some of the other tests awaiting them.

The first day was designed as a hard physical slog so we could have a look at the group and so they could have a look at one another working and to see who was contributing and who wasn't. The subsequent debriefs around the team exercises were reasonably open but it had no significant impact on them as they'd been there and done that type of thing before.

We then sat round and had a discussion that centred on how they might be described by their opponents, say Port Adelaide, which was easily the most successful club in the SANFL with, at that stage, over thirty premierships since 1870. How would they see us?

We sent the players off in small groups and asked them to come back when they had some words down. They returned with what amounted to a long list of derogatory terms; 'soft', 'front runners', 'easybeats', 'undisciplined', … and so it went on.

We then asked them how, in a perfect world, would they want their opponents to see them? The responses were interesting in so far as they didn't talk about winning games or premierships so much as gaining their opponents' respect, something they obviously weren't getting much of at the time.

What we'd done, very simply, was identify the gap between how the team was and how it wanted to be.

If they're seen as soft and undisciplined when they actually want to be respected, then it poses a range of questions: What's holding them back? What is it that's stopping them from being respected? What is it exactly about their current behaviour that doesn't engender that respect?

They identified issues that might be contributing to the lack of respect they were getting; things like their approach to training, poor match preparation, an inability to hold up under pressure and a lack of off-field discipline, which, when it was boiled down, amounted to too much alcohol too often.

We got them to come up with the kind of behaviours they felt they would need to improve on to become a more respected team. To be respected more, they decided, they needed to train better, be better prepared for matches and to be more disciplined off the field. We wrote it all down on a sheet of paper and pinned it to the trunk of a big eucalypt.

We finished off the day with a very hard physical exercise and when they got back I pointed out to them that I'd spotted over near the barbecue a very large pile of ice-cold beer cans. They were pleased about that but a little concerned. What were the rules concerning the beer? How would they be disciplined about it?

Discipline? 'Do we have any boundaries?' I asked them, 'Do you have a code of behaviour?'

One of the senior players said, 'Ray, we're at a reasonably elite level of football. We can just use our common sense.'

I questioned that player a little further about what that meant and made the point that for some players common sense meant one thing and for others it meant another. There were as many versions of common sense on the camp as there were people. Common sense, I said, is not as common as some people think.

I didn't want to trick them into anything so I warned them that tomorrow would be a pretty solid physical day and we'd be getting underway fairly early in the morning

There were some more discussion and a decision was made that they'd finish the drinking by eleven o'clock and go to bed.

I asked them if that was it? Would there be, say, a limit on the number of cans each player drank? A senior player said, 'Ray, blokes should know whether they've had enough or not so let's not go overboard with it, let's just let the guys make their own decisions about it? But at eleven o'clock, we finish.'

Luckily we had enough cans to last well past eleven o'clock.

~

THE COACH AND I WERE HAVING A CAN OF BEER together when eleven o'clock eventually came. Alan stood up, on his way to tell the players to finish their cans and to head off to bed. 'Oh well,' he said. 'It's eleven o'clock, I'd better ...'

I cut him off mid-sentence. I told him that the only person he had to look after here was himself; he'd look after himself, me myself, the players themselves. The best we can do is manage ourselves properly.

The players, I said, made a commitment today that they wanted to be more respected by being more disciplined and preparing better. One small step in that was to go to bed at eleven o'clock and to be in good nick tomorrow morning. If they're going to improve as a team, they needed to be able to manage themselves and before that could happen they had to be allowed to manage themselves. In the end they'd only follow their own rules, the ones they actually believed in, so we had to let them set their own rules and see if they were any good at it.

Alan begrudgingly headed off to bed, not entirely sure if it was the grog and not the leadership trainer talking. I did a quick check to see there was no possibility of the players running out of beer and climbed into my sleeping bag.

The noise told the story.

Many were still drinking after midnight.

One, two and three o'clock passed and there was still a lot of activity.

I got up at four o'clock to see what was going on, which was plenty. The senior players—the leaders, or role models some might say—were the only players left, and some of them were in an advanced state of drunkenness. Some of the coaching staff, including Peter Jonas, were with them, just in case, we learned afterwards, anything should go wrong. The players, of course, saw the coaching staff's presence as a licence to continue drinking, which raised the issue of self-management I'd spoken with Alan about at eleven o'clock. In this case, they didn't stop drinking and go to bed because, well, not everyone stopped drinking and went to bed.

I spoke with Peter and gave him my take on the situation, half-expecting, perhaps, that he'd tell me to get lost. He heard me out and said, quietly, 'I will never do that again.'

~

WE WOKE EVERYONE UP shortly after dawn with the help of a saucepan and a soup ladle. I love the sound of clanging metal in the mornings, almost as much as I do the endless groaning of badly hungover footballers awakening to a new day. Some were in such poor shape they weren't sure where they were, and quite a few more were sheepish, probably waiting for my response. In the normal cycle of football club behaviours, after they'd somehow misbehaved they'd somehow be punished and that, in theory, would balance the ledger.

We started a warm-up but a couple of senior players were so sick they simply couldn't do what was required.

We went back and sat down in the dirt around the campfire and I asked them how they thought the camp had been going? Initially the senior players were in control of the discussion: 'Yeah, it's been pretty good,' they said, 'We've bonded together well.'

Of course, bonding together well meant they'd got to drink a lot with their mates. The older blokes drank with the older blokes, the younger blokes drank together, and so it went on. There wasn't any breaking down of barriers between the subgroups within the team.

Their replies continued on in stock-standard fashion until one of the younger players said it: 'Ray, this is bullshit.'

Bullshit? That's the magic word to a facilitator. My training kicked in and I swung into action. 'Go on,' I said.

'Yesterday afternoon,' the young player said, 'we all committed to being a team that would be respected. We said we'd be disciplined, that we'd be more prepared … '

He went over to the list pinned on the gum tree and went through it, point by point, just like a coach would normally have done. But this was far, far more important than anything the coach could have said. This time it was coming from a player and, in particular, a young player. Someone in the playing group was challenging the team's status quo. 'I just don't think that we're even serious about this,' he said.

Some of the senior players sensed trouble and entered the fray trying to defend themselves. 'What would you know, you've only been here five minutes?' Then the finger pointing started: 'At least I didn't drink as much as him', and 'Yeah, but he can drink more than you and still play better than you anyway …'

The point they'd missed—and in my role as facilitator it's the one I brought them back to—was that if winning this particular argument meant they could keep doing what they'd been doing, then nothing had changed and they were still as 'weak', 'soft', 'undisciplined' and all the other things they'd said the previous day they didn't want to be any longer. It wasn't an argument worth winning. If things were going to change, they'd have to look at it differently.

'If Port Adelaide had a videotape of our night last night,' I asked them, 'Would it have convinced them that this team isn't soft, undisciplined, front-runners? How would that behaviour look to them? Would they respect what they saw?'

The senior players became even more defensive and difficult, so much so that one of the younger players suggested that maybe this was just a waste of everyone's time.

I made the observation that we'd just been through a learning experience. So where did they go from here? It was their team and their issues, no one else's, and their behaviour was the key to it. If they didn't change their behaviour then how could anything change? The club would simply continue the trend of the last thirty years, bringing in optimistic new coaches with their new rules to bang their heads against the wall for a few years before the club spat them out, older, wiser and sadder. Nothing would change.

Perhaps, I said, the players should sit down and decide among themselves whether to pack up and leave the campsite and, if they wanted to, take the remaining beer and drink it back at the clubrooms. Or they could take seriously the discussion we had yesterday and try to move forward.

Alan had some reservations. He thought they might decide to head back to town with the beer. If they did, I said, he would know sooner rather than later that he would never have been able to turn the team around because if there weren't a majority of players dissatisfied with the position the club was in and were prepared to act, then nothing would change. As it happened, the group decided to stay and work, which was a great illustration of how the weight of numbers is critical in any change process.

~

INSTEAD OF MAKING RULES about their behaviour, we were asking them, 'How does this behaviour look?' and getting them—the team members, no one else—to compare that with the way they said they wanted to be seen. I was pushing the notion, as I had been all weekend that the players make decisions for themselves. Rather than the coach saying, 'There will be no alcohol at the camp', or 'There will be alcohol but that this is how we'll do it', or 'You must stay here at the camp because that's the rule', it was important to throw the issue back to the group and make them decide for themselves how they'd handle the situation and, therefore, take ownership of their own rules and, more importantly, their own behaviour. Thus, the players' decision to remain at the camp obviously carried far more weight with them than if the decision had been made for them.

What did we learn from the weekend? For a group with issues surrounding alcohol and self-discipline, the night-time activities provided us with more information to work with than the physical challenges we'd carried out during the day, and the coaching staff and players became roughly acquainted with the notion of how the team taking 'ownership' of its values would work in practice.

It had been a successful weekend but it was clear the framework was going to challenge everyone's preconceptions, players and coaches alike. The players weren't used to the idea of making their own calls about how they behaved, let alone policing it themselves.

For the coaches it was a paradox because the history of Australian football and team sport in general was steeped in tales of stern, demanding coaches extracting optimal team performance. And here I was telling them that the best way to improve the team's performance was for the coaches to take several steps back and allow players to become far more engaged in the design and application of standards for their team. For a pre-season camp, maybe, but it would take an enormous amount of faith and courage for football coaches to commit to the framework when the serious business of football begins.

I was more confident than ever that the ideas applied to a football team but I was also prepared for the news that Alan Stewart, Peter Jonas and Peter Vivian had, like the RAAF outside of AAFTS, decided it was a bit too radical for their football club. But, as I've learned time and again, they are brave men. Either that or they didn't have the heart to tell me to nick off.

NO BLAME, NO EXCUSES

THE CAMP WAS A TERRIFIC INSIGHT into who the potential leaders were among the young players, who in the group was genuinely committed and where the deadwood might be, and afterwards Alan had a much clearer idea of the personnel at his disposal in terms of changing the club for the better.

Behavioural change doesn't happen immediately and just because we'd had that discussion out in the bush, it certainly didn't mean that everyone jumped on board straight away. Alan was patient, knowing that the rate at which players engaged would be different.

In the meantime we had to help the team identify who its real leaders were. Who was going to lead them to where they'd said they wanted to be?

Contrary to a lot of the players' initial expectations, that certainly wasn't going to be me. It took a little while but everyone eventually understood the difference between my role and the black magic and chicken-liver men football clubs had been known to employ in their darkest hours. I wasn't going to be doing anything that might help them win games, that was entirely up to them. There'd be no hypnosis, ouija boards, pep talks or casting spells over the opposition; all I could do was help them, the players, begin taking responsibility for their own performances. I'd be challenging their superstitions, not encouraging them.

So who in the group was going to lead the team? Who best reflected the team's aspirations? The Australian football tradition is for those who'd played the most games or were the most gifted footballers to be the designated team leaders—the captain and vice-captain and, maybe, a deputy vice-captain. As I saw it, if the team said it valued seniority and talent, then it ought make those types of players its leaders. But if the Central District players wanted to be more respected and saw the way to achieving that respect was to be more conscientious at training and to prepare better for matches, then the club's leaders had to selected by that criterion.

And why only two or three leadership positions?

From what I knew of teams, any team of twenty or so that relied on just a few of its members to lead the way nearly always went poorly, whereas the leaders in successful teams weren't so obvious because there were so many of them. If leadership can't be left up to just a few then the conventional structure seemed to me to be sending the wrong message, if not to the captain and vice-captain, then to all the other players.

Why is it done that way? Because that's the way it had always been done. It's an odd leadership structure that's best ignored it if the team's going to work effectively.

For a team to be successful then there had to be as many leaders as possible—a leadership group rather than a few individuals—so why not reflect that in the structure? Obviously there has to be a designated captain at matches because there are important duties to be performed like the coin toss and asking the umpires at half-time why they're crucifying the team. But anyone who demonstrated the qualities the team valued was surely a leader, irrespective of how many games they'd played or their football ability. So why not acknowledge it?

The players nominated, including the captain and vice-captain, ten players to the club's leadership group. Those players attended some leadership training sessions on awareness of leadership styles, developing a leadership code and team-building skills.

~

ONCE WE HAD A LEADERSHIP GROUP that reflected the team's espoused behaviours, we needed to set up among all the players an open and honest feedback system to enforce those behaviours.

We knew from the research into failures of teamwork among aircrews that the first symptom of the failure was invariably a lack of communication about a problem which then sets off a chain of events and misjudgments that can end with investigators hunting for a black box. Even when we have a framework of behaviour, and in the case of aviation a supposedly failsafe one, sometimes transgressions will go unchallenged because a person doesn't think it is their right to do it. But by just letting things go and not communicating their observations effectively, a team member is effectively saying, 'Oh well, I will just look after myself from now on.' And if team members were only taking responsibility for their own performance, then it wasn't as good a team as it could be.

The feedback system usually employed around football clubs—and plenty of other places—is humour or sarcasm. Overlooking the fact that over the years there's been a hundred million riotously funny lines delivered 'half-jokingly' in the vicinity of football clubs, if the stakes were a bit higher than getting a kick it'd be easier to recognise it as being a very dangerous way for a team to communicate. If they were crewing an aircraft it might be enough to get them killed.

The idea behind half-joking—humour, irony, sarcasm—is that if someone hears the same cryptic message often enough they will eventually get the message loud and clear.

It doesn't work, of course, as the messenger is avoiding taking responsibility for their message. If the recipient ever stops to think about what's been said, they then have to work out whether the other person was serious or not and, if so, if there's any truth in what they've said. They can never work it out on their own and if they do ask, 'What do you mean by that?', they'll get in return, 'C'mon mate, I was only joking.' No one learns a thing.

At Central District, the initial changes to the culture revolved around the development of trust, honesty and accountability for both the coach and the players. We wanted every player to be able to say without fear to another player that 'You didn't do this well enough and you need to improve' or, conversely, 'I accept that I didn't do that well enough and I need to improve.'

As the leadership group developed the players began to take more responsibility for developing training drills and match strategies, areas that were normally regarded as the coach's responsibility. This sharing of responsibilities had one obvious impact on the playing group, which was to heighten their expectations of one another. That, in turn, led to greater individual accountability.

On his part, Alan took the long view and resisted the temptation to focus on doing whatever was required to win the next game, or even the one after that. All kinds of coaching decisions, whether it was match day selections, promoting youngsters or delisting players, were guided by the team's trademark. If that meant the most talented footballers weren't always in the team or, sometimes, no longer at the club, the players all knew exactly where they stood because they, the players, had set the criteria Alan was using. They might have been a little surprised initially when Alan adhered to those principles as strictly as he did and was so courageous in their application, simply because it's an extraordinarily rare football coach whose ideals can't be seduced and then compromised from time to time by outstanding football talent. In that regard, Alan was unimpeachable; players identified with the team's objectives or they weren't in the team, no matter who or what they were. Every hard decision he made sent a powerful message to every corner of the club, and to the rest of the competition, that things had changed at Central District.

~

FOOTBALL IS A SMORGASBORD of excuses for teams and individuals not wanting to take responsibility for their own performance. There's umpires, the weather, injuries, the venue, the coach's strategies, team-mates' mistakes, the shape of the ball or, when all else fails, plain old bad luck.

As the season progressed and the team settled into its new ways, it was confronted with an old demon—'Norwood at Norwood.' It doesn't look so bad on paper but they were words spoken in hushed tones at Central District. The club hadn't beaten Norwood at the Norwood football oval in eleven seasons and as the match approached the club regressed into blame and excuse mode as one horror story after another emerged about the terrible things that had happened to Central District over the decades on the killing fields at Norwood. Young players who'd never played at Norwood must have been dreading the prospect of going there, irrespective of it being a football oval much like any other.

In the week prior to the game we got the team together to discuss the issues around not having won at Norwood for so long. Some of the senior players weighed in with their excuses; it's a small ground, there's fluky winds, they're a tougher team on their home ground, and so it went on. Win at Norwood? Not likely. They'd turn up, get their backsides kicked and go home.

I suggested there was really only one option then and that was to ring up the SANFL and tell them the team was facing reality and would forfeit the match. The reason? We weren't prepared to take responsibility for our mental as well as physical preparation so we'd be turning up at Norwood knowing for sure we'd get beaten which, in reality, is forfeiting. Appearing to turn up for the game was a deception. It would be better, I said, to make it official and save their team-mates, the coaches and supporters the disappointment of the team just turning up there and going through the motions like they had in recent years. We could use our time more productively going to the movies, or catching up on the gardening or with friends.

The players' reaction was interesting. For some it was confirmation that I was, in fact, a peanut the coach had picked up off the floor at the pub. But the main response was indignation, which was a good springboard for further discussion.

We broke the bundle of anxieties down into parts and one by one addressed each issue as a real problem and the players decided on some strategies to deal with each of them.

With those mental hurdles out of the way, it was eventually agreed that there would be no excuses and the team would not only turn up at Norwood that weekend, they would all turn up to play. There was no talk of winning but there would be no talk about losing either. Above all, whatever happened, there would be no excuses.

Being largely concerned with process I try to be dispassionate about results but I was very happy when they won at Norwood. There was no denying the significance of the win, it was the evidence the players needed to reinforce that if they could take responsibility for own their performances then they could take control of the situation.

While the team was obviously pleased with the win, there was none of the wild celebration that might have been expected after breaking such a long drought. They hadn't relied on an act of God—it rained because as a team they'd made it rain. It's a different emotion. And for some players the result would have had some very big question marks hanging over it. Having seen what happened when some of the barriers to good teamwork are removed, it would have got a lot of them wondering about how many matches had been lost previously because the team had talked itself into losing long before match day.

I could see the barriers were coming down and the possibilities opening up in the players' minds. Maybe they were and always had been a better team than they'd thought they were?

~

THE SEASON HAD given us a good look at how the players were responding to the framework and the football club was going to have to decide which way it wanted to go philosophically. That is, was it going to go with the leadership and teamwork principles we'd set up or would it revert to standard football club procedures. It was time, as they say, to make the hard decisions.

What does a struggling football club do with footballers who either won't or can't fit in with the culture the club wants? It's a question that gets to the heart of the old adage about 'the team comes first'. How exactly do you put the team first when you have someone who is producing outstanding results while behaving contrary to the team's values?

Alan Stewart was now deeply committed to idea of making decisions according to the team's values and decided he was going to reward the players by those standards. Not unexpectedly, given the club had been down for so long, the financial situation was particularly tight so and if there were going to be any pay rises at all the following season they'd only be marginal. Alan decided that aside from some small pay rises for four players who'd been identified by the peer evaluations as having performed extremely well in team-related areas, he was going to keep the remainder of the team on the same pay they had been the previous year.

One high-profile player indicated he was not going to accept the situation. He wanted more money. It was explained to him that Central District were playing a very different game to the one he'd known for so long. The team had decided they were willing to make individual sacrifices for the team's success and this season one of those sacrifices was not receiving as much money as they would have been hoping for. There was a finite budget and increasing one player's pay necessarily meant reducing the pay of one of their team-mates. No one had to accept it and anyone was free to leave if they were unhappy about it.

'I know what you're trying to set up here,' he said, 'and that's okay. All I want is a bit more money ...'

It was a huge dilemma for the club because it didn't have any ready-made replacements and Alan didn't want the integrity of the framework undermined by the typical football club solution to keeping the star player happy without ruffling the other players' feathers by finding a benevolent member to quietly slip the star the extra dollars.

Instead, Alan consulted the leadership group and gave them a full account of the situation, sharing with them all the financial details and all the other considerations he'd taken into account in deciding how the money would be spent the next season. The players were stunned that their team-mate was so unwilling to make the same pay sacrifices they had but, more importantly, they accepted the logic and the long-term benefit of aligning their remuneration with the team's values and how this might well cost the team one of its better players. The players in the leadership group made it clear that if push came to shove and their team-mate wouldn't relent, Alan should hold his ground.

The unhappy player was given another opportunity: 'Look, we've pushed it right to the edge. If you want to keep the respect of your mates you will fall into line with them and you'll go out there now and train with them. If not, you'll go to your car and leave knowing that you aren't coming back.' He went to his car and left.

While he'd been mouthing the right words and appearing to play the team game for a couple of seasons, in the end he confirmed that values the team had decided upon, with his input, were actually secondary to him wanting an extra twenty or thirty dollars a week. The only pity about it was that if he hadn't gone on with all the unnecessary guff about mutual sacrifice and commitment to the team's goals, the club could have accommodated him with a transfer to a wealthier team much sooner.

Given the team-oriented demands of the framework it was always a strong possibility that there would be a high-profile casualty. Some footballers are professional in the strictest sense of the word in so far as they play for the money and the highest bidder wins, and there's absolutely nothing wrong with that as long as it's clear to all concerned.

Even though losing a good footballer was regrettable, the way the club approached the situation was, I thought, a big step forward. Every other player was observing the situation and how would it have looked to them if the club had caved in to the player? What was being rewarded here? The team's values or freakish football talent? Had it been the latter, it would have reduced the team's values to something written on a bit of paper and so far as culture change went the club would have been back to the drawing board.

There were no losers in the end. The star found a club willing to meet his financial demands and he rewarded them with several years of good football, and Central District's team performances improved markedly in the wake of his departure. The team's improvement obviously couldn't be put down solely to Alan's decision to let the player go but it was, nevertheless, a significant factor. Managing the situation the way he did sent a powerful message to the team that its values remained intact, and this in the long run has far greater benefits than any one player can bring to the table, no matter how good they might be out on the ground.

Outstanding individual talent might hold sway in, say, golf or tennis, but the numbers work against it in a team sport like football that has eighteen players on the field because, all myths aside, there hasn't been a footballer born with enough individual ability to compensate for the negative impact they can have on the rest of the team's performance if the player's goals and the team goals are not one and the same. Managing all players effectively—and effectively includes losing some of them—has to be preferable to going down the slippery slope of bending, and thereby undermining, the team's values. Believing the myth about the match-winning superstar and bending to their demands will cost a football club dearly; far more than any financial considerations involved.

We learned at Centrals that only when a team has been confronted with the decision and, above all, made the right call, one that's consistent with its trademark behaviours, can it get over the morbid fear that in the absence of a particular player their team will cease to perform.

~

THERE WERE SOME positive developments at Central District but, as we learned, there was still plenty of the old culture hanging around. Well ahead of schedule, and somewhat unexpectedly for the club and the rest of the competition, Centrals made the finals at the end of 1993. The club was filled with hope. Maybe they could go all the way?

The answer came soon enough and the team were eliminated in the first week. The playing and coaching personnel handled it well but the reaction around the club was interesting as people hung their heads and bemoaned that nothing had really changed and that the future looked like it would be just like the past.

The young Central District players were, in effect, being burdened with a history they had no part in and we had to do a lot of work with the players to make absolutely sure they understood why this was happening and the strategies they would have to use to combat it.

~

I CONTINUED THE WORK with Centrals while still working full-time in the air force running the leadership and teamwork development training. Every day was another practical lesson in the nuances of team dynamics and my downtime was spent immersed in books and papers on the subject. I saw there were resonances in what we were doing in all sorts of writings, from Greek philosophers to Civil War military strategists to W. Edward Deming, the so-called 'father of quality management'.

On the one hand, I shared many of their conclusions about the effective leadership and teamwork. But we'd converged on the Pole by different routes. Others had the underpinning principles down pat but how the principles apply in practice is left largely up to the reader. Or where there was some direction about what to do next, it was complicated beyond my comprehension. The process we'd used at Central District for the team to take ownership of its values and behaviours and improve its performance was, compared to some of the alternatives, like a two-man tent against the Sydney Harbour Bridge.

I could see that the benefits Central District were reaping were similar to those that businesses obtain when they'd successfully embraced a quality management program but, given the literature, I thought, a values-based framework as simple as ours must be too simple for the business arena or someone else would have tried it already.

The club's on-field improvement eventually sparked interest from some of the club's sponsors about my running some team-development and culture-change workshops with their staff and I jumped at the opportunity. As I'd suspected, the principles applied to sales and marketing teams and tradespeople as well.

Like the football teams, the way they wanted to be wasn't always how I might have predicted it. Salespeople value sales about as much as football clubs value premierships, but, like football clubs, that's not all there is to it. Trust, integrity and respect matter to salespeople too so, like the football teams, we went through the process of working out how they would have to behave to achieve that respect. And just like the football teams, when the sales teams took ownership of their code of behaviour their performances improved.

SAME GAME, DIFFERENT GOALS

AS CENTRAL DISTRICT PROGRESSED and we began to see unmistakable changes in the club's culture I was already thinking about how the framework might apply in different situations. I decided that the next step would be to try it in another sports environment, this time the one I was most familiar with—country football and netball clubs. It would test the model in all sorts of ways as the purpose behind country sports clubs is, ironically, much more complicated than merely playing sport and trying to win. The clubs are a focal point for a range of activities, embracing netball clubs and in some regions hockey clubs as well and, as I knew, their social role in the community was every bit as important as their sporting function.

A friend from university days, Gerard Fitzgerald, was back in Victoria teaching in the Western District. Gerard ran a farm at Derrinallum as well as teaching full-time at Mortlake and to give him something to do with his spare time he'd taken on the senior coaching job at Mortlake, a club in the highly competitive Hampden Football League.

Back then, Gerard was probably most famous for his three games for Geelong in 1977 and being mentioned in dispatches at 'sportsmen's nights' ever since as the young player who was to be introduced to the umpires before a game by his captain, John 'Sam' Newman, but the captain didn't know his team-mate's name. There's a lesson in there somewhere about leadership style and team success and you can work it out for yourself.

I'd rung Fitzy frequently to keep him posted on how things were panning out at Central District and he eventually relented and let me run a camp with his players where we could go through some of the concepts that we'd been exploring at Central District.

We went through the exercise with his players: How do we want to be seen as a team? What sorts of things are important to be that sort of team? What sorts of commitment are we prepared to make to be in the team? It was a revelation, seeing how, with the minimum of facilitation, the players' belief in one another increased as they made agreements among themselves about how they would approach their footy to enhance their chances of success.

The feedback from the camp was extremely positive and if I wasn't convinced already that the framework was an incredibly useful tool for teams of any description, I was only a couple of experiences short of it.

That work with Gerard's team led to a series of workshops with other country sports clubs that were some of the most rewarding work I've done, a universe away from the semi-professional SANFL clubs, which were themselves far from well-heeled but still light years ahead of the bush footy clubs in terms of funding, resources and personnel.

~

SMALL COUNTRY TOWNS have always done it hard but it's never been harder than the last few decades. For some football clubs confronted with dwindling local populations, survival has been a matter of one amalgamation after another and constantly reconfiguring leagues to keep competitions viable. It has never been easy organising a football match but it has never been harder than it is nowadays in the bush and for all the glamour and glory of the MCG with a hundred thousand people packed into it, Australian football's best asset has to be the legion of volunteers who keep country football clubs alive, doing countless hours of unpaid work on administration, maintaining their ovals, sheds and netball courts, arranging transport for the juniors and preparing and donating food that can be sold to the spectators so the teams can buy new jumpers every few years; doing whatever they possibly can, no questions asked, to make sure their teams make it through another season. You'll hear it time and time again around country football clubs, 'Oh well, I suppose we just love our footy around here' as explanation for the extraordinary community-driven feats that are necessary to field a team.

At least I understood exactly what kinds of issues country clubs struggle with because, unlike Maritime Patrol Group missions or playing sub-elite football, I'd been there myself. Country football clubs were more than somewhere to get a kick. People can pick up anything from bookkeeping to building maintenance and event management skills at a football club. Or they can, like me, just have a good time around the club and work on their social skills. It all counts, it really does.

First, the clubs looked at what was important to them. No football club rejects the idea of a premiership but more important than the on-field achievements for a county football club is being able to sustain the club for what it really is. And that's so much more obvious when you are in a remote town with a population of three hundred people and 150 of them are there at the club having a few drinks and a meal together, kids running everywhere. If that scene could continue forever without the football team ever winning another game, then there'd be no great loss to humanity. And how would a succession of premierships tally up if winning them meant the club were no longer fulfilling its role as the social hub for the community? As we learned, at country footy clubs the social fabric always prevails over flags.

Clubs obviously have to be administered well and have responsible people making sure the club goes forward and achieving whatever its on-field goals are, but above all that it delivers on the other parts of its mission of being central to the town's social life and providing its people with the opportunity to grow and develop in whatever their role was with within the club.

If the clubs were going to be around for a long time, they had to behave like they were going to be around for a long time. Sustainability had be more than a word, they had to put it into practice. We'd identify the threats to their sustainability—issues like too much being left to too few—and work through the reasons behind it. If people were reluctant to take on key roles because the roles were simply too demanding for most people, then they'd create some new positions, redistribute the workloads and learn to delegate. If people felt unable to help, it wasn't due to laziness, it was because they weren't confident they knew what to do. Basic training would be arranged for several people at a time so there'd be an abundance of that skill when it was required down the track. They began succession planning so people were familiar with practices and procedures long before they'd started in their jobs, and when they did assume the position, that they understood how important it was to the club's best interests that they in turn trained their successors.

~

ONE NIGHT I WAS AT A CLUB going through the concept of identifying the kind of club they wanted to be. I spoke about motivation and how that was up to them, and that the group must decide what it wanted and then decide what it was prepared to sacrifice to get it.

The whole team and much of the community were there and, as is often the case, the bar had been kept open while I spoke. I noticed this particularly large bloke had stayed down the back of the room for the duration, taking advantage of the opportunity to have the bartender largely to himself.

Towards the end of night I invited some questions from the audience and there were some good ones. We talked through the various issues raised and worked out some strategies they could use to address them.

Eventually the big bloke down the back thrust his hand into the air. I thought he might have a question but as it turned out it was more of a statement: 'Ray,' he said, 'It's really struck me, this idea of sacrifice and I'm committing to everyone here tonight that, for the rest of this season, on the night before a game, I will drink no more than ten pots.'

The crowd erupted. People stood and applauded, children danced around him and old men went over and shook his hand. It was obviously a bit late to meet his target this particular night but the commitment was made and to those present, this was clearly a significant undertaking, as if he'd donated a (well-worn) kidney.

I was a bit sceptical, thinking he'd be highly unlikely to remember it the next day let alone follow through. But, I heard later, he was a man of his word. He'd knuckled down to a rigorous ten-pot regime, his performances on the football field improved and he became quite a valuable player for the team over the next couple of seasons. It confirmed to me that performance improvements are most definitely relative. And, of course, that one person's self-management can look like exactly like another's binge drinking until it's put into its proper context.

The big bloke's ten-pot a night pledge has stayed with me as a full-colour illustration of how the framework can be useful on so many levels. People don't have to live in a cave and eat roots and leaves to get some benefit from it. And the knowledge that—in certain circumstances—ten pots of beer can lead to performance improvements hasn't hurt me either.

~

AFTER A FIFTH IN 1993, Central District ended up third on the ladder in 1994 and qualified for the finals again. There was an increasing tendency for the team to follow through on their commitments and since they'd said all season that they'd learned from the previous year's events, their reaching the finals was less of a surprise. Still, the club wasn't entirely used to the idea and there remained a lot of superstition around the place about 'fate' and 'destiny' determining football matches. Centrals then played Norwood in the first semi-final and won by four points, their first win in a final in twenty years. Winning finals didn't fit with the Central District pattern so this was a bit different. Maybe things could change? Maybe they'd already changed?

The talk around the club was reinforced by the media also hammering the point that things seemed different around Central District nowadays, though outside of the administration, coaching staff and the players, very, very few people had any real insight into what was really going on. We certainly weren't being secretive about the model but there was a general disbelief that a football team could improve itself significantly if the players talked and related to one another differently, so that was usually regarded as well-rehearsed cover story to conceal the real truth. A young team, a controversial team structure, going behind closed doors for hours at a time, then improved performances? Other clubs whispered about crystals, faith healers and goat's head soup. We didn't bother discouraging that because while the opposition were speculating about black magic they weren't fully concentrating on what they ought to be doing and that would work to Centrals' advantage. I thought they were queuing up to fill the gap Centrals were going to leave around the bottom of the ladder.

As it happened, Centrals bowed out in their next final but afterwards the mood around the club was hopeful, even buoyant. The team said they would learn from it and go one better next time and that was good enough for the members and supporters. It wasn't for me to talk them down as the team was setting its own goals but, still, I wasn't sure how realistic they were being given the club had never actually made it to a grand final. At the same time, it wasn't like they were saying they could fly off the top of the grandstand, in which case they'd have to be told they were overreaching. All I knew was that if enough of them had a genuine expectation that they would make the next grand final then they may well, whereas if enough of them were harbouring doubts about it then they most probably wouldn't.

BREAKING RANKS

I KNEW I WASN'T GOING TO BE HAPPY going off somewhere else in the air force to another training role, but one way or another I would be transferred out to do my time at radio school or as a librarian because I'd already pulled every available string to stay on at AAFTS and the pressure to move on was steadily increasing. And now I knew which area I wanted to work in, doing anything else seemed to me like a gross waste of time. I began to think, or hope, there might be sufficient demand for the kind of training I was providing to make a business of it.

The move from teaching to the air force was significant because it decoupled me from the generational link with teaching and the Education Department, but the RAAF was a still a government job and financial security was guaranteed. I was acutely aware that stepping from the air force into my own training business was a world away from that and would require a lot more forethought and learning some of the lessons from the previous move and making sure I applied them this time. I communicated openly with Sally and she became very much a part of the planning process. She understood the kind of work I'd been doing and had ideas on how that might translate into a 'training consultancy'. We were both acutely aware of the risk, going from a comfortable salary to nothing with three kids under five.

~

MY LATTER DAYS IN THE AIR FORCE taught me a lot about how people think and what drives people because the overwhelming advice that I was getting from people about leaving the RAAF was that I was mad. Why would you leave the air force? One person said, 'But all you've got to do is stay upright and breathing and you've got a job for life.' I imagined the epitaph; 'RAY STAYED UPRIGHT AND BREATHING ... UNTIL NOW' and, I thought, this bloke ought to be a motivational speaker. I took note of his technique and went away more determined than ever to get out of the air force, and sooner rather than later.

It was unusual to find someone at work who was positive about the move. Under the superannuation scheme, after twenty years you're eligible for a lump sum and a pension and everyone was waiting for that magical time before they headed off to do whatever it was they really wanted to do, something I would certainly advocate to people if they're in a position to get a payout. But not if it means working unhappily as a librarian or teaching at radio school for fifteen years until it happens.

Another colleague got my attention when he said, 'What a great time to go and start a new business. You've got a wife, a young family, you've got a mortgage, you're putting everything on the line. You can't afford to fail.'

Of all the advice I'd received, this rang truest to me. If I put everything out there, I knew one thing for sure and that was that I'd work as hard as I possibly could to make it work. Whether that would be enough was hard to say but on the strength of the work I'd done with the aircrews, footballers and sales teams, all of which had been successful, I was confident I had a good 'product'. But how would I go selling it? Sally would think of something, and it'd give her something to do when she wasn't juggling three children under five. Thus, we decided we'd begin our own training company based around 'a values-based approach to leadership, teamwork and culture change'. That's what we wrote down anyway. We even had the perfect business name, 'Esprit de Corps', or what would have been if we'd spelt it phonetically or had been selling to the French.

I'd been open to the idea from the very earliest days of working at AAFTS that the results we were getting from such a simple framework were an illusion. But it had passed every test we'd thrown at it. So I was comfortable about the decision in the sense that I was passionate and motivated about what I'd be doing because I genuinely believed in the product. We'd find a way to make it work.

The RAAF had been good for me and I'd write my own letter this time: 'Dear Air Force, I won't be at work today because my hobbies have become too interesting.'

~

WE PACKED UP AND HEADED BACK TO Victoria, looking for a home that would put me in range of the sports clubs I already had a relationship with. We settled on Ballarat, where Sally and I had met at teachers' college, and closed the circle on a journey that had begun when we'd been handed our degrees nearly fifteen years earlier and taken us up to Stawell and Donald, down to Point Cook and then over to Adelaide. It was good to be home. Ballarat is an hour away from Melbourne, we're close to the Western District and the Wimmera–Mallee, and not too far away from Melbourne Airport so I could get back to Adelaide in a couple of hours.

In the early days of the business, people would typically ask, 'How is it going?' They really meant, 'Are you making any money?' Well, yes and no. Sally was working in a milk bar to keep us afloat so that was the 'yes'. I was generating contacts at a furious rate and the signs were positive but income was a little harder to come by. My relationship with Central District remained intact and I was still catching up with Gerard Fitzgerald and the country football clubs were keeping me busy but it still wasn't enough to pay the bills.

We were working out of a home office in Ballarat in a Victorian 'restoration project'—a cynic would have said a rundown old shack—and going through the unpaid but necessary routine of priming the business pump was challenging. Most mornings I got up and spent three hours on the phone cold-calling businesses and schools to see if they were interested in a leadership program. A what?

I hadn't expected a good income immediately but it was a harder road than I'd planned on. We were trying everything we possibly could to make it work. I was randomly sending letters off to businesses, challenging them with, say, 'How to you think your teams are performing? Could they perform better? How well are they led?' and trying to stimulate some kind of interest. I followed up the letters with telephone calls, stumbling along getting different responses, me making little sense of them and them of me. I was building resilience and a nice patter on the benefits of leadership training but not much of a business.

Football clubs and coaches at all levels, including the AFL, got letters from me explaining how the program had benefited Central District and why I thought it might be applicable to their teams. I'd ring afterwards to see what they thought. They get a lot of letters from people with ideas to help the team.

I sent off a flyer to some businesses I'd picked out of the telephone book and to my surprise, about two or three days later one came back by return mail from a personnel manager at a large hardware chain who said, in short, it was the biggest pile of garbage he'd ever seen and that my flyer made me sound like an 'out-of-work public servant', which was fair enough given that I was exactly that and hadn't, until then, felt particularly ashamed of it. He went on and gave me some tips on what he thought I should have said in the flyer, scratching out my words and replacing them with his suggestions.

Getting that kind of feedback when you're a couple of months into your new business leaves you a couple of choices. One is to curl up and die. Or you can do what I did, which is curl up briefly and then try to remember some of my own principles and put them into effect. So I rang the writer to let them know that I valued their feedback and to thank them for, rather than just throwing my flyer in the bin, taking the time to let me know that they felt there was a better way. They were as surprised to hear from me as I was from them and we had a productive discussion and I was given some names that ultimately led me to paid work.

That flyer incident reminds me about the importance of being able to receive feedback. If I'd shown to him that I was annoyed and angry with him because of the feedback, I would had to have shut up shop that day. Nor did I mention to him that I thought his ideas would have made me sound like an out-of-work clairvoyant.

Work began trickling in, one-off sessions here and there from sports clubs, schools, insurance companies and real estate firms. Every session was another learning experience for me, not only about how the leadership and teamwork framework panned out with different groups, but also in how best to meet the expectations of the customers and deliver the information effectively.

Towards the end of the first year of the business I got a call from the principal of Donald High School, Brian Brazier. Brian asked if I could come back to the school to run a team-development session with the teachers based around the principles I'd been developing. There hadn't been a lot of staff turnover in the six years since I left and my first inclination was to say no. The prospect of fronting up to a group who would still have vivid and occasionally nauseating memories of me as a teacher and giving them a sermon about personal responsibility and commitment to the team was, unlike us, a bit rich. Brian mentioned payment and I said he'd caught me at a good time.

I decided honesty would be the best policy, which was going to be a novelty for me in that environment. I'd acknowledge my past and throw myself at the mercy of the group. Maybe then we could get on with business?

'You might remember me ... ,' I said, 'as being the first man to the pub and the last man home ... for enjoying social functions too much ... spending too much time reading the form guide ... for being directionless ... for snoring during staff development sessions like this one ...'

I told them I hadn't come back to lecture them or tell them what to do and that I understood that the level of professionalism they may have seen from me in the past might not have been ideal and I hoped they could understand that as I'd been developing this behavioural-change business my own behaviour had somehow changed.

We went through the process: What is the real purpose of this team? What kind of team did they want to be? What kind of behaviour would get them there?

As with the aircrew and the footballers, I couldn't give them any advice on how to do their jobs better so much as alert them to the possibilities of what might happen if they could find ways to share with one another the vast collective knowledge their team already contained. We set up some principles they could use to guide them and some structures that allowed them to gather meaningful feedback on their performances in an environment where people felt it was okay to speak honestly.

Afterwards we headed off to the pub and I could tell there was some anticipation about my transformation when the beer kicked in. But it must have been a moonless night because nothing happened. We caught up, I had a couple of beers and thoroughly enjoyed myself. I bade my farewells and headed off back to Ballarat and the Donald police moved their terror-alert status back to orange.

Some of the teachers must have been disappointed that I hadn't lived up to the legend, and the publican would have been devastated. Most of the feedback from the teachers was, nevertheless, positive. Personally, it was a worthwhile experience because for all my reminding old teaching friends and colleagues of some highly regrettable incidents they were remarkably accepting of my efforts to change. Some said they actually preferred me without the malt and hops vapours.

Marching in on The Saints

Don't be afraid to take a big step if one is needed.
You can't cross a chasm in two small jumps.
DAVID LLOYD GEORGE

I'D FIGURED THAT IF I WAS EVER going to get a response from an AFL club it would be from one of the strugglers because they'd obviously be more receptive to the idea of change than clubs with recent memories of success. There'd be no pressing need for Hawthorn, Carlton, West Coast or Essendon to be fiddling with cultures that were already capable of delivering premierships. The most likely takers would be a club that, like Central District, had had a gutful of trailing the pack and were receptive to radical measures.

Along with fifteen other AFL coaches, I'd sent one of my letters to St Kilda coach, Stan Alves, who'd been in the job for six months or so when I wrote to him in 1994. From where I stood, the Saints didn't look to be going particularly well and seemed to have cultural similarities to the old Central District. There were some extraordinarily talented high-profile players, there'd be heightened expectations with each new coach and each new season and the team would fire up at random times and look like they might be contenders. Briefly.

The cycle had been running in overdrive at St Kilda for nearly twenty years, and Stan was their tenth coach since 1976. The average St Kilda coaching stint since then had lasted about thirty-five games, or seventy hours of playing time—about the same time the average tail gunner over Europe in 1943 could expect in their job before they were hosed out at the end of a mission. If feeling secure about your situation is a condition for optimal performance then it's no wonder St Kilda's coaches had struggled.

Football club cultures are generally flint-hard and can resist change for decade after decade as the old induct the new into the club's ways, then the new grow into the old and repeat the process. But the AFL clubs really are in a whole other league and they're tougher than diamonds. For the AFL clubs out of Victoria it's a continuum unbroken by wars or pestilence for over a century, and reinforced by the reporting that makes sure nothing's ever forgotten. For example, newspaper reports from the 1890s and 1990s, and probably every decade between, have praised the Geelong team's skilful play while bemoaning its supposed aversion to physical contact. The mythmakers send no apologies when they're proven wrong; instead, they credit themselves with highlighting the issue and inducing the turnaround. Then the moment the team goes off the boil the allegations resurface with new vehemence. Nothing changes but the dates.

For St Kilda the perceptions have been different, in some ways the opposite of Geelong. Physical contact was in abundance at the club, on and reputedly off the field, and for years it had supposedly turned its home ground at Moorabbin into bog to reduce the skill gap between them and their opposition, whoever they were.

There were enduring question marks over the club's off-field culture that was notorious for its lackadaisical approach to football. It went all the way back to the late-1800s when St Kilda teams might not even turn up for matches if they thought an afternoon at the Caulfield races held more appeal. Then as now, the club had a reputation for, on their good days—and there weren't too many of those—being able to take on the best teams in the competition and humble them, irrespective of their positions on the ladder.

What St Kilda really excelled at through its history was bitter infighting among the team, the club administration or both. Allan Killigrew, the Saints' coach in the late-1950s, told *The Herald* in 1980 that 'they had a tradition but it was a horrible one. They were losers. You'd have thought they were playing football for laughs, there were so many playboys and buffoons around the club.' Things had changed but not enough because Moorabbin was perpetually in crisis. They were in no man's land.

Club loyalties have tempted over the years a steady stream of movers and shakers—prominent businessmen, racing identities, politicians—to put their people skills and reputations on the line, and sometimes their money, to try to change AFL clubs' habits. They'd march in bubbling with positive energy and, in all but a handful of exceptions, get carried out on a stretcher a few seasons later, their pockets turned inside out and mumbling about people being so unkind.

Between the Saints' solitary premiership in 1966 and Collingwood's in 1990, Carlton, Essendon Hawthorn, North Melbourne and Richmond shared all twenty-three flags between them. The other seven clubs, the majority of the competition, settled for losing the majority of the time. At any given time one of the stronger clubs had usually dropped away briefly and a weaker club surged briefly, but the tale was essentially the same year after year as clubs like St Kilda, Footscray, Fitzroy and South Melbourne survived on increasingly dim memories of past glories, the latter three having to look even further back than the Saints to their most recent premierships, in 1954, 1944 and 1933 respectively. For their coaches, often club champions drafted back to the clubs to salvage the situation, coaching could be a living nightmare, a death by a thousand insults as they're held responsible for being unable to create successful, winning cultures.

The Australian Football League, which was the Victorian Football League until 1990, was a different animal to the twelve-team competition I'd planned on playing in back in the 1960s and 1970s when six games were played simultaneously on a Saturday afternoon and the collective television coverage of the four television networks amounted to a couple of hours a week. Back then, eleven of the clubs were based around inner-Melbourne and Geelong, an hour down the road, was the outpost.

Changes were afoot in 1981 when South Melbourne started playing all its home games in Sydney on Sunday afternoons to glean the benefits of exclusive television coverage, and then ended up as the Sydney Swans. Several other Melbourne clubs were considering relocation if that was their only chance of survival, while at the same time the VFL was canvassing the idea of expanding the competition to incorporate interstate clubs and becoming a national competition to ensure its own survival.

The situation limped along until the Brisbane and West Coast football clubs were admitted in 1987, then Adelaide in 1991 (and, eventually, Port Adelaide in 1997). Those first three interstate AFL clubs were started from scratch, without history nor culture to assist or burden them, and they were expected to be competitive against clubs with the knowledge and wisdom accumulated over a century. If proud clubs like Fitzroy, Footscray and St Kilda could only manage one premiership a century, what chance would the new chums have?

For the Victorian clubs, it was like shock therapy. By 1994 the new interstate clubs were already eclipsing some of the Victorian clubs' lifetime achievements. West Coast made the finals in its second season, a grand final in its fifth season and premierships in its sixth and eighth. Adelaide went within a hair's breadth of making a grand final in its third season. The struggling Victorian clubs could look to Sydney and Brisbane for reassurance that there wasn't something in the Victorian water but those two clubs were obviously sleeping giants with huge population bases to draw supporters and revenues from to buy, if not better players, then better facilities and more support staff. When they started winning they might never stop.

The AFL was doing its utmost to keep the competition on a so-called level playing field. The teams were subjected to a salary cap and there was a draft that advantaged the less successful teams.

The AFL's objective was to give every club in the competition a fighting chance of being successful if they managed their players effectively, and therefore every opportunity to remain viable business concerns in the long term.

With the equalisation measures in place, the clubs had to learn how to squeeze every last drop of performance from their players. The players' physical conditioning became firmly based in sports science, the skills, strategies and tactics of the game mapped, analysed and dissected like never before. Clubs used statistical measures of team performance, nutritionists, sports psychologists and professors of human movement, the draft candidates' prospects kept in confidential dossiers and each club carries out intricately detailed research on their opposition. Everyone watches everyone else trying to see what their advantage is and trying to replicate and, hopefully, better it. There are no patents or copyrights and industrial and athletic espionage is the order of the day, so whenever a club finds success using a particular approach, half a dozen of the other clubs will latch onto it immediately and the rest soon after that.

~

WHEN I WROTE TO Stan I questioned the club's culture and outlined the precepts behind the framework and how they might help, and said that I would call him over the next two weeks to make sure he'd got the letter. After about three weeks of going through in my mind not so much what I was going to say to Stan but what Stan was probably going to say to me, I picked up the phone.

Just make the call? Ring an AFL coach and say, 'Look, I think I can be of some help to you in improving the performance of your team and your club.' Some would say it was drawing a very long bow. I sat down in my office in Ballarat and made the call. I spoke to Stan. He agreed that it would be useful for us to catch up.

It was a telling moment. Was I serious? Did I really believe I could help an organisation as complex as an AFL club? I suppose I must have as I was only too aware at the time that a high-profile fiasco might well stop the business dead in its tracks and I was still keen to go ahead with the idea.

I drove to Melbourne in mid-1994 to meet with Stan and we spoke at length about what we'd been doing at Central District and how it might apply to St Kilda. I had some examples of success indicators from the RAAF and Central District to show him. Stan was reasonably interested but the Saints were one of the most under-resourced AFL clubs and there was no possibility of my doing any work for them at that stage.

Stan and I kept in contact with regular telephone conversations during the second half of 1994. The club finished that season thirteenth out of the fifteen teams and Tony Lockett, the club's marquee player, left and went north to Sydney. The football community reached a consensus that without Lockett the club would not just fail to improve the following season, it would get worse.

Finishing where it did on the ladder, St Kilda had several early draft picks and recruited some talented young players. The club reviewed its management structure after trying to get by without a chief executive officer by distributing that work to board members, and Don Hanley, who'd been working with the AFL, was appointed to the position in late 1994.

Soon after I was invited to a meeting, an interview or a trial run, I wasn't sure, but I was told that a room had been booked at the Carlton Crest Hotel for four hours for me to outline the program and why I thought it would be useful to St Kilda. Present would be Stan Alves, Don Hanley, Gary Colling, Trevor Barker, recruiting manager John Beveridge, and the chairman of selectors, Kelvin Moore. Put into its proper context, I'd followed Australian football from birth and would be walking into a room with several Australian football legends who had played about a thousand games between them and they would be waiting to hear what I had to say for myself. I had to remind myself not to be intimidated, that my program should be the focus of the meeting, and to not ask for autographs.

West Coast had just won its second flag by eighty points over Geelong and there was an air of gloom, perhaps even desperation, over Victorian football. I drove to Melbourne, my mind wrestling with the details of the presentation and trying to imagine how I might behave if I hadn't been in awe of the audience. I arrived at the Carlton Crest around eight o'clock in the morning. They were all there.

What was I going to do to assist the improvement of the players? When you're talking about improving an organisation, if you only attack it at the grassroots level it's like a management team in a company saying, 'What are you going to do to fix the workers?'

I asked them: 'Well, how do you guys go as a team?'; 'How would the players see you as a coaching team?'; 'What sort of behaviour do you model to the players?'

The keynote of the session was that if the club embarked on a Performance Improvement Program, which was what I'd begun to call the program because you have to call it something, it would have to be the administration and team managers as well as the players. If it was a cultural problem we had to address the culture, not just the team. There was no bag of tricks to improve the players, the team or the club. It was a process of becoming a better club, and no shortcuts or pretending.

That four hours was invaluable. It probably left the club management with more questions than answers but they got a sense of the structures I was recommending; to set a destination for the players, get a clearer set of player behaviours and standards, and to establish a senior leadership group that had autonomy and had some input on managing the playing group. I might have mentioned Central District's third-placing in the SANFL that year.

A week or so after the Carlton Crest Hotel summit, Don Hanley got back to me to let me know the club had found ten thousand dollars and were willing to take me on as their leadership consultant for the 1995 season. I accepted the offer with both hands. But the money was insignificant compared with the incredible opportunity it presented to test the model in the most challenging team sports scenario in Australia. It was like being given permission to test some home-made tyres in a Formula 1 motor race.

~

As I'd done with Central District, the process at St Kilda started on a pre-season camp, in this case at Lorne, a coastal tourist town along the Great Ocean Road on Victoria's west coast. With restaurants, hotels and ice-cream parlours, it was a bit of a contrast to Palmer in the Adelaide Hills and a fair reflection of the difference in SANFL and AFL clubs' spending power.

Stan introduced me to the players on the Friday night before we set off. I briefly told them my background. I asked them about themselves, about what they get out of football and what they hoped to get out of it by the end of their careers. They wanted a premiership.

I got the five players who were twenty-eight years or older to stand up. These people, I said, were the only ones in the group who were even alive when St Kilda won its solitary premiership in 1966. None of them could have any memory of it. That premiership was worlds away.

We talked about the club's history and the unpalatable reality that of the fifteen hundred players who'd represented it at the senior level, only twenty of them had ever participated in a St Kilda premiership. That, in the context of a team game, ninety-eight per cent of St Kilda players walk away empty-handed. Perhaps they were on the wrong train here if they wanted a premiership? They'd have to be very lucky.

I told them about a sign I'd seen in the sheds at a country football club that, to me, summed up their situation perfectly. The sign said 'ONE IN—ALL IN', and across the bottom of it someone had scrawled '*until the shit hits the fan and then it's every man for himself*'.

The danger for them, I said, was that if any one of them had ceased to believe that their team goal, a premiership, was going to be fulfilled at St Kilda, then they would do what came next and cease to pursue those team goals in favour of their individual objectives—playing two hundred games, kicking a hundred goals or finishing near the top of the club's best-and-fairest award—which are admirable achievements in themselves but are not, in the end, why they play the game. They are compensations for a lack of team success, not a path to it. And it was those kinds of attitudes that were holding the club back. The only people with the power to change the team's fortunes were they, the team. They would have to decide what they wanted, decide what they were willing to sacrifice, set their priorities, and go out and get it.

Their performances, I told them, were a product of their attitudes, habits, beliefs and expectations, all factors that were within their control. In the end it was up to them and the expectations that they had of one another that determined their collective fate. Quite simply, if they raised their expectations of one another their standards would rise and their performances would improve accordingly. Football is about the weight of numbers, like forty players fighting over twenty seats on a bus, and the weight of numbers explains the ebbs and flows of a football match. The scoreboard is merely an indication of which team is occupying the most seats at any given time. Every player who gives up their seat—in other words, is being beaten by their opponent—makes the fight so much harder for their team-mates to sustain. I'd seen in the newspapers how the Saints were supposedly struggling with their newly adopted ground at Waverley Park. If, I said, only a handful of the team had begun to believe that, then the team's lowered expectations of itself were a self-fulfilling prophesy.

We explored some of the excuses St Kilda might have been accepting as a group. The usual football suspects were identified—the weather, umpires, injuries, the shape of the ball, bad luck, the coaches blaming the players, the players blaming the coaches, the forwards blaming the backs, the backs blaming the forwards—and we looked at how those might be affecting their match-day performances.

How often had they turned up a couple of men down? How many matches had been lost because, long before the opposition had laid a bump on any of them, they'd talked themselves into accepting defeat? What if everyone had turned up ready to play? And everyone had known that everyone else was ready to play? Would that have made a difference? Maybe they were and always had been a better football team than they'd thought they were?

If they were going to take responsibility for their own performances, the group would have to leave the land of blame and excuses behind them and enter a different world where honesty is the norm and stuff-ups are learning opportunities.

They were all superb footballers. After all, they'd all made it to the AFL and you had to be bloody good to get on the radar screen of an AFL club, let alone be recruited or ever play a game. But were any of them so complete a footballer that there weren't areas of their games that couldn't be improved?

They were in a great position to do something about it. They had at their disposal the collective knowledge of forty elite footballers. What if they could learn to share all that knowledge among themselves? If individuals became even slightly better players, then how could their team performances fail to improve? And with the AFL so competitive, marginal improvements counted.

They, the players, would be the brains behind the operation. They were going to help identify one another's strengths and weaknesses and then help one another improve in the areas they were deficient in, and that meant every area that affected them as a team.

Around football clubs, feedback is usually couched in terms of 'praise' or 'criticism' but they would have to learn to look at it differently. How could they improve if they didn't know where they could improve? For all our self-awareness as people, we spend our entire lives confined within our own bodies and none of us ever gets to observe ourselves in action. How else, if we don't gather feedback from other people, can we ever know how we present to other people? No one wants to hear a list of their deficiencies but if they could see feedback more dispassionately, as something they could take or leave without any 'shoulds' attached to it, they might pick up some useful information. Don't argue, just hear it out and go away and think about it.

Whether their performances improved or not would be directly related to their ability to accept feedback from one another and that would require of them a different kind of courage to that they displayed out on the football oval.

Nowhere to Hide

THE LORNE PRE-SEASON CAMP included some physical work but the bulk of the time was spent establishing the underpinning values and behaviours that we referred to, for want of a better word, as their 'trademark'. We probably could have called it their 'hallmarks' , 'imprimaturs', 'Saints-traits' or 'team-endorsed behaviours'. But we didn't, we called it their trademark.

The team was the usual mix of personalities and AFL experience. Among the established players were household names like Nathan Burke, Danny Frawley, Robert Harvey, Stewart Loewe and Nicky Winmar. There were young guns like Justin Peckett and Peter Everitt who'd been there two or three seasons, and there was a younger group that included Joel Smith, Austinn Jones, Tony Brown, Steven Sziller and the Wakelin twins, Darryl and Shane, all players who were at the very beginnings of their AFL careers.

Similar to the Central District process we explored what kind of team they wanted to be and what kind of behaviour that would entail. There was a general recognition that they needed to be more disciplined, more committed, work harder and so on, which was nothing new to the team or me. They were the typical observations about improving a struggling team that anyone—the players, the coach, supporters, Blind Freddy—could have made. They would have heard it a couple of hundred times from Stan and he'd only been there a year.

We spoke about regaining some of the respect from the competition and being more successful, again the typical aspirations of a team. If that feels like déjà vu and it's all been said before, it probably has. But it's not all right to save time by bringing along the last group's piece of butchers' paper. Involving the team members in the process of identifying what kind of team they want to be puts teeth in whatever it is on that piece of paper and that helps learning later on when it comes back to bite its authors on the backside.

The first night of the camp a group of the senior players did their bit for Lesson One by going out for dinner then drinking too much and returning too late.

We returned to the city and I called the senior players together and asked them how they felt the camp went. They were happy enough: 'Yeah, we did well, got to know the young kids …'

'Try to put yourself,' I said, 'in the position of some of these young kids that we have brought into the system. Have a think about what they saw? We said we wanted to be a more respected unit, a more professional unit, more disciplined, all those sorts of things …' The first impression the young players got was of a group that talked about being professional and then immediately showed that they weren't serious about it by having too much to drink and staying out too late, to the extent that it affected their next day's training.

A couple of the players were particularly disappointed by the situation because they were, in fact, exceptionally professional and the young players' first impression was not at all representative of those senior players' normal behaviour. Unfortunately though, I said, their 'cutting loose' coinciding with their first meeting with the young players so forever more those young players' earliest memories of the club would be of the team's leaders being completely bonded.

In Australian football, I explained, the setting of directional goals had always been considered the coach's charter. When I entered St Kilda I was told the players were not interested in involving themselves in managing their own team, they just want to train and play football. Was that true? To improve, I said, we had to bring teams and individuals within the teams back to accepting responsibility for what they said they wanted, not what the coach said he wanted, and that was the significant shift that would be occurring at their club.

'If we can develop an environment where each player has a vested interest in the development of his team-mates, and people are driving themselves individually and collectively towards the team they want be, the team's performance will improve and continue to improve.'

They looked sceptical. How many AFL games had this bloke played? It might have been better, I thought, if they'd heard it from one of their team-mates. Or another athlete. I should have mentioned the marathon.

~

SINCE BEFORE JOCK MCHALE coached Collingwood, football coaches have supposedly had to be hard men, scarier than the opposition and capable of intimidating their players into playing better football. As the game's strategy and tactics evolved it's allegedly become even more of a coaches' game, the players seen as chess pieces to be manipulated from above. It's a straightforward system; the coach runs the show and if it works out badly the coach identifies the reasons behind it and if the reason is in the playing group, he comes in and punishes the group until learning appears to have taken place. It's a military idea and a military outcome, the 'leave your brain in the bucket by the door before entering' approach where homogenised players do what they've been told to do even when they know there may be a better option. If leadership is seeing something, knowing what to do and then doing it, expecting people to 'dumb down for the sake of the team' is its dead opposite.

The framework we were introducing challenged the autocratic coaching style and required a particular kind of courage from the coaching staff and administration to relinquish the reins and hand responsibility for the team over to the team. It was so unconventional compared with the normal run of things at a football club that even when people understood the framework and its benefits and the need to behave and make decisions consistent with the team's values to reap those benefits, they'd still baulk at hard decisions it throws up.

I'd seen it at country clubs where they hadn't been game to follow through because no one was game to tackle a particular player or issue, not because they didn't think it was the right thing to do but because they'd sooner not. And a few compromised decisions later they'd be right back where they started, wondering why nothing ever seemed to change. It only takes one or two opportunistic decisions to brand the club's shot at cultural change as another brief flirtation with some new ways.

Stan was already inclined toward a values-based framework before my arrival on the scene and it wasn't as big a stretch for him as it would be for some to grip the levers lightly. He agreed to be bound by a decision-making framework based in his team's trademark behaviours and to put his faith in the collective intelligence of his players. He certainly understood the broader life issues and had a perspective on football that allowed him to put his players' best interests at heart and he was also very open to the idea that a values-based framework at the club could benefit not only the team now but the players later on, once they'd moved on beyond football.

~

St Kilda got through the pre-season and the team nominated a leadership group that reflected its values, but for a while there it looked like the framework was a purely theoretical exercise we'd completed on the camp that had no real impact. Nothing had changed. There was, nevertheless, the usual pre-season football club talk of all the signs pointing towards a better year.

The first game was nearly three thousand kilometres away in Perth and there was little shame attached to losing there. The next game was at home against Richmond and the Tigers were seen as vulnerable … but they weren't. The flogging in Adelaide hurt, as did the loss to Hawthorn at home and the twenty-goal hiding from Essendon. But nothing stung like losing to Fitzroy, who were in extremis and about to be put down by the AFL.

From the media commentators' jaundiced point of view, there didn't have to be smoke to report a fire. The evidence was all circumstantial: the Saints weren't travelling too well, the Saints' coach had done his thirty games, the Saints often sack coaches about now. If it all goes well for the news outlet, they'll unnerve the club administration into equivocating for a millisecond over a response and then there'll be a series of 'PRESSURE MOUNTS ON COACH' headlines or pictures of the coach at training captioned 'DEAD MAN WALKING?' It's scurrilous and it can temporarily wreck lives for no good reason but it sells papers so the situation isn't going to change in a hurry.

Well-founded or unfounded, if the 'coach under the pump' talk goes on long enough people can begin to believe it, and if key people begin to believe it then the coach is dead in the water. It's the worst kind of self-fulfilling prophesy and once it's done its work no one really knows why it happened because no one really knows what to believe about what everyone else believed at the time. All they know for sure is that once the talk started it was very hard to stop.

There's only one way out and the key is honesty. What exactly are people saying and what are they actually thinking? A crystal ball won't reveal that, nor supposition.

I thought it was time we sat down and looked at our team's behaviour and the supposed new direction we'd taken in terms of

trademark behaviours and being more honest about our performances. I asked Don Hanley if we could convene a meeting of the
key board members, the president, the director of football, the key
football staff including the coaching panel, the football manager
and the half a dozen senior players in the leadership group.

The topic for the meeting was, nominally, an assessment of
Stan as a coach. We set the room up so that Stan was at the front
and there was a semi-circle of chairs around him. I asked those
present that all that was required of them was an honest response
to the key review questions.

I asked if anyone had been spoken to about the coach's
performance. Everyone answered in the affirmative.

Had they spoken to anyone else about it? In other words, had
they initiated a conversation about the coach's performance? Most
indicated they had.

'Has anyone spoken with the coach about the coach's
performance?'

No one had.

Thus, I said, this would be a good opportunity to give Stan
some of that feedback. He would sit there, say nothing, and hear
what they'd heard and what they'd said. I acknowledged to them
that it was a difficult exercise but it was either that or continue on
the way they were going, with the usual outcomes.

There were a range of suggestions and criticisms. Stan heard
them out. As soon as they'd delivered the feedback I thanked
them for their attendance and let them go.

Stan was extremely frustrated that he hadn't had a right of
reply. But as I told him, one of the most important things in

allowing people to give feedback is that if you accept it without defending yourself, sometimes they'll go away and think about their behaviour rather than yours. Whereas, if you defend yourself against criticism or counter-attack and say, 'But what about you?,' it gives them the opportunity to conclude, 'This was supposed to be about their performance and they didn't listen. I'm right after all.' Being grateful for the advice disarms the person who delivered it. And you never know, there might be something in what they've said that might be worth knowing. You can make your mind up about that afterwards.

In the wake of the meeting the coach and the senior players resolved not to discuss their performances with other people and to work together.

~

NOW IT WAS TIME to get serious with the players. We'd been referring on occasions back to the type of team they wanted to be and its trademark behaviours but it hadn't been referred to all that regularly and when it was, it was having minimal impact on some of them. I decided it was time to really challenge the group by embarking on a peer evaluation process.

I prepared a sheet with all forty-two players' names on it, assembled the team in the change rooms at Moorabbin and gave each player a pen and a copy of the list.

The players were asked to put their names at the top of the page, scratch their own name off the list and to then rank their peers in terms of who best lived and modelled the team's values and core behaviours, from one to forty-one.

'We said these behaviours were important but we haven't said how important we think they are. Let's find out how your team-mates think you're going with it and you can discuss it with them.'

The exercise was much more difficult than the players had first thought. There was nowhere to hide.

One player came to me during the exercise and said, 'Ray, I'm philosophically opposed to this exercise.' In his mind the process would be too confronting and too hurtful to his team-mates. In my mind, he'd realised he was about to find out unequivocally where he fitted into the group, which was the very point of the exercise.

There was no denying it was a tough business and there were numerous risks associated with it. But the alternative was to keep going the way they had which was the way it had always been. We had to trust ourselves to manage the process so that it wasn't just a witch-hunt without follow-up or support.

I collated the information on the sheets through the following week and a number of interesting things happened. One was the consistency of the ratings. The same names were always in the top ten, and in similar order. Likewise for the bottom ten or fifteen.

When I first suggested the exercise, the coaching staff said it would be of limited value because the only thing we'd be likely to learn was who got on and who didn't because the players would simply look after their mates.

Well, as it turned out, they didn't. In the bottom ten we had some big-name senior players, as well as players who were indisputably very popular among the group.

And in the top ten were two really interesting names. One was Rod Keogh, who'd been delisted by Melbourne before Stan had brought him over to St Kilda. Rod was quiet, he came in, worked hard and went home. It would have been easy to mistake him for a journeyman but, as we'd learned from his team-mates, he exemplified the team's espoused values and the example he set was a strong positive influence on the younger players. He was, in fact, a leader.

Another interesting inclusion in the top ten was Tony Brown, who at that stage was a seventeen-year-old yet to play a senior game. He was a leader too.

To bring the issue into focus, I went back to the team and asked them why they'd ranked their team-mates the way they had, since there was so little correlation between the rankings and a players' age or experience. If the question is simple and the answer self-evident, it hadn't been so obvious to them until then. Phenomenal talent or ten years at the top level weren't to be sneezed at. But those weren't the team's values. The behaviours they'd said mattered around here were being open and honest, having a strong work ethic, not cutting corners, having a positive, enthusiastic attitude and never making excuses. That's why Rod Keogh and Tony Brown were high on the list and some of the team's most accomplished players were down the bottom.

Over the following weeks we worked our way through with the playing group as to where people had been ranked and why they'd been ranked where they had. We sat in a big circle where there was no stepping back from what was said.

Keep in mind that this was back in 1995 and none of the players had been through a process anything like it so they had to learn the ground rules.

Firstly, the feedback had to be depersonalised. Every participant needed to understand that we were talking exclusively about behaviours—about what people *did*. If someone were to say 'I do not like your behaviour' it must not be heard as 'I do not like you'.

Feedback had to be delivered positively and set against the behaviours the team had decided it needed to adopt. More importantly, any feedback had to include a strategy for improvement and a commitment to support the player in their efforts to improve.

The latter condition, a commitment to support their team-mate, was probably a redundancy as it seems that very few people can look someone in the eye and tell them they're doing something wrong without then wanting to show the recipient of the advice how to do it right.

I'd made it clear to the players throughout my involvement with them that we all operated by the same rules and that I could only do a good job if I got honest feedback about my performance. When I got home after the first peer-review session, the answering machine was loaded up with messages from players. The feedback was largely positive, which was gratifying because we'd taken a risk on the exercise and it seemed like we might have introduced something the players saw as useful.

One player said it was the first time that he could recall the team being genuinely honest with one another and that he could see how a lot of good could come from it. That gave me reason to pause and think: Here was a player late in his professional football career and the implication was that, in all his years at the top, he'd never been a part of a playing group that was capable of the kind of honesty that permits team-mates to sit face-to-face and tell one another, 'Listen, I think you can do better.'

Like anyone else around a football club, he'd have heard plenty of muddled information being exchanged couched as humour or sarcasm, but there's not much honesty in that and it doesn't give the recipient much to work with. In our feedback sessions there was no laughter or punches in the arm to confuse the message, and no one had had a good time in there. But at least the players now had a solid idea of what they had to do if they were going to improve.

We saw a couple of responses from the players who were told to lift their game.

One response was to drift away from the group and do nothing. In that situation the options are very narrow. All you can do is explain to them exactly what the story is, and that the feedback and commitments of support from their team-mates was about the best opportunity they'd ever get to improve as a footballer. If they elected to do nothing and were delisted at the end of their contract, they couldn't blame the coach or anyone else as they alone had behaved their way out of the system.

That's a harsh message but it is far better for players to receive it while they still have the opportunity to remedy the situation. Too often players are called in by the coach and told they've been delisted and the reasons for the decision. And, not unreasonably, the players respond with 'but if you'd done the right thing and told me that earlier, I could have done something about it.' People need feedback if they're to improve their performance and there's nothing to be gained delivering that feedback to them at the wrong end of their career.

The other response was a positive one, and a number of players implemented the improvement strategies that had been suggested to them and began to improve. Among those was Peter Everitt, a 200-centimetre twenty-one-year-old ruckman in his third season of AFL football who was very much relying on his extraordinary natural talents to keep him in the game.

The theme in Peter's feedback was that his work ethic needed to improve, and there were also doubts expressed about his commitment to football. Initially I was concerned that he might find the process too hard but he was far tougher than I'd guessed because instead of sulking or giving up he began to work hard and it was fascinating to watch him improve the way he did over the next two or three years.

~

TONY FRAWLEY, THE REGIONAL MANAGER for the Ballarat Rebels under-18 side in the elite Victoria State Football League, and Ian Baker, the team's inaugural coach, adopted the framework in 1995 and his replacement, Garry Fletcher, persevered with it. Kelly O'Donnell, the coach of another under-18 VSFL team, the Murray Bushrangers, also adopted it, as did his successor at the

Bushrangers, Xavier Tanner. By now the program was getting a fair old work at just about every level of Australian football and it seemed to be holding up all right.

Over in South Australia, Central District was participating in its third successive finals' series and made it through to its first-ever SANFL grand final appearance. Port Adelaide won it comfortably but there were no excuses from the Centrals players, just a determination to learn from the experience.

Grand finals generate some strange and unusual emotions that challenge football clubs in all kinds of ways. Win or lose, the hardest things to do in the wake of a grand final are the things that got a team there in the first place. If winning breeds arrogance or complacency that manages to reduce the team's performances to mediocrity afterwards then it's hardly a victory at all. And if the disappointment of losing generates waves of recriminations and negativity or what-ifs, one less premiership cup in the cabinet will be the very least of the club's problems as it tries to go forward. Whatever the match result, if it's not used as a valuable learning experience then it's a lost opportunity.

Centrals coped better than could be expected and hope prevailed over disappointment at the club's post-grand final function. There were no complaints. The coaches and the young team had taken the club into uncharted territory and it was a better place than Centrals had known previously. They'd look at what worked, what didn't and how they could do better next time. It was a beginning, not an end. Or so we'd thought.

Alan Stewart took the microphone and announced he was moving on to do what he thought he did best which was identifying young football talent, and that he had coached his last game. He'd made the decision some time ago and hadn't mentioned it to a soul so it wouldn't distract the team from the task at hand. The room fell silent for a few moments as the crowd digested what it was hearing. Then, led by some sobbing from over in the corner, it erupted into some of the loudest and most forlorn wailing you'd ever want to hear.

The pain wasn't over yet. Peter Jonas was lured back to the AFL by his former North Melbourne team-mate, Malcolm Blight, who'd taken over as the Adelaide Crows' coach at the end of 1995, and Peter was appointed the Crows' runner. Having done all the groundwork to lead Centrals out of the wilderness, it now looked like neither Alan or Peter were going to be there to share in the successes that would surely come now the club had got its act together.

In other environments the departure of two key coaching staff might leave the club directionless until the situation sorted itself out. It would be an interesting test of the model Centrals had adopted. Could the club continue to build a successful culture or would it fall away in Alan and Peter's absence? Time would tell.

ON THE WHOLE

THE WORK WITH CENTRAL DISTRICT continued, as did my relationship with Gerard Fitzgerald's teams, and word-of-mouth was providing a steady stream of school and corporate work that our flyers had failed to attract.

Working with elite athletes in the AFL, the only slightly less elite SANFL players, and then the country footballers, I was struck by their very different situations. They were all young men between, say, fifteen and thirty-five years old, and the Central District and country footballers would have given away one of their senses to play at the top level and earn the kind of money and recognition AFL players do. Yet it looked to me like the AFL players were in a trap.

Around 1994–95, as I was getting involved with St Kilda, the AFL was entering a new era as the players made the transition from part-timers to full-time professional athletes. Until then most players simply hadn't been able to earn enough from the game to consider it as a full-time job and consequently had to find other paid work to keep their heads above water.

As the league made its transition to a national competition, its revenue base increased markedly and the interstate clubs and a couple of the wealthier Victorian clubs raised the bar. For the players at the interstate clubs, the frequent travel made other jobs impractical. And while the travel situation was slightly more manageable for Melbourne-based players, the rehabilitation and recovery sessions were becoming a daily task and clubs were scheduling training at all hours, timed to prepare the players best for whenever and wherever their next match was, local or interstate, night or day. The players' football income increased accordingly, in recognition that their football commitments largely precluded them from taking on other jobs. But football was still only a part-time commitment and players were left with a lot of time on their hands, and no lack of money to keep themselves entertained.

For the players it might have been a luxury if the risks of being raised in captivity weren't so high. With their alternative careers on hold until they'd finished with football, most of the players who were recruited to the AFL after 1994 were never going to know what a regular job was outside of football until they were outside of football, nor would they have the friendships and relationships previous generations of footballers had in the community to fall back on when their playing days finished.

From where I stood, it looked like the modern footballer was being, in effect, institutionalised. The game was largely all-consuming while they were in it but sooner or later they were all going to be flung out into the real world. When the Nintendo-trained footballer left the game it would leave a much larger hole in their lives than it might have for footballers in the past. And the

AFL was already awash with stories of former players who'd failed to make that transition from the heady world of football to everyday existence. That situation was only going to get worse.

For a lucky few that day of reckoning might not be until their early thirties but the average AFL footballer manages only forty-five games—two seasons—so there'd be some extremely insecure young men around football clubs now and in the future. They'd either make it as AFL footballers or it would be oblivion, and if they made it in the AFL it might well be oblivion anyway. For any particular player the edge of the cliff was as far away as their contract extended and that was rarely more than a year or two.

I knew that for a team to do its work effectively the individuals in it have to feel secure enough in their overall situation to be able to serve the team's goals ahead of their own individual interests. Yet here was a professional team sport that was inadvertently structuring itself in a way that actually militates against optimal team performances.

At any time there are 650 or so AFL players, with roughly a fifth of them being turfed out of the system at the end of any particular season. To where? Where was the superannuation, the vocational counselling, the retraining and all the other mechanisms that needed to be in place for an individual to be able to go to work and give one hundred percent of themselves to the team? If I were a professional footballer I'd be too worried about growing old or getting injured to be thinking about what the team most needed from me to help it win a premiership.

The players' career structures were out of my league. However, to their credit, the AFL Players' Association and the AFL were working on a number of strategies to address this situation. In competitive terms, it was only a minor hurdle because St Kilda's performances would be measured relative only to the other teams and there were no other clubs out there making any great inroads into tackling the players' lifestyle predicament. So while I was confident the Performance Improvement Program would still have a positive effect on the team, I was wondering how much we were missing out on by putting the players in such a flaky situation and how much better performance we might get from them if every player was secure about not just their role in the team but also about their post-football futures? So their football focus could shift from 'me' to 'we'? It was a very, very big question and not one I felt I could answer.

~

St Kilda, I thought, were in a similar situation to the one Centrals had been in back at the beginning of 1993. They would have to make real inroads into their culture before they could make any inroads into the competition.

A values-based framework is not, as much as some people would like it to be, a quick-fix solution to losing football matches. It's not a game strategy or confidence-boosting hocus pocus, it's a tool for cultural change and only once the culture has actually changed can there be any genuine improvement in the team's performance. Winning a match is not evidence of the framework's success, nor is losing evidence of its failure. Those events happen whatever the club's culture. A far better indication is how the team handles winning or losing. How does the club deal with success? Does it learn from failure? What kind of people is the club developing?

The most pressing cultural issue that has to be addressed is attaining systematic honesty about the team's performance. Secondly, the coach and players need to be able to assess which of the players are genuine about continuously improving and which players are harbouring themselves in the system and avoiding the sacrifices that are necessary for them to improve their skills.

And it's not just about football skills. Football clubs get confused between winning and success, and they get even more confused between talent and character. Typically, great footballers are feted, good players get looked after, and ordinary players often receive ordinary treatment. Its by-products are socially dysfunctional 'superstars' and cynicism and disillusionment, but that's the landscape many clubs find themselves operating in. Clubs are forever saying people who pass through them leave in better shape than when they arrive. From what? The bonding, presumably.

Everyone buying into everyone else's improvement is crucial. To have a professional attitude, train hard and prepare well is all well and good. But if team members don't look up and see what's going on around them, then the team's performances will fall short.

To improve, players have to develop broader skills in terms of communicating with their team-mates, being able to deliver and receive feedback, being able to set goals for their own improvement, and acknowledging that setting a direction in not only their football, but life outside of football, will benefit the team and the club it represents.

~

ONE COMPONENT OF THE LEADERSHIP TRAINING I was delivering concentrated on communication skills within the group. Such is the size of a football team, addressing the group is in fact a public speaking exercise. And we know how many people feel about public speaking. Footballers are no different. Some are quite comfortable with it but most would prefer a forearm to the head.

As was the way of football clubs at the time, if a player could speak well in front of a group, that was good. And if they could get a kick as well, then they were a budding captain. But if a player wasn't comfortable with a crowd, well that was just bad luck and there was nothing a football club was going to do about it. Players might receive some rudimentary media training where they'd learn to say 'hopefully' or 'just looking forward to next week' when they really meant 'uuumm' or 'aahhhh', but the object of that training was mainly to to prevent players from underperforming because they were worried about dealing with the media. Far from encouraging the players to express themselves in any meaningful way, the players were trained to say precisely nothing. Which, of course, is how the clubs liked it. Who knows what these idiots might say if they start expressing themselves?

It was indicative to me of how little football clubs were prepared to invest in their own people. While there was a clear recognition that public speaking was a leadership skill and that leadership skills helped win football matches, it was left up to the recruiting people to find those skills because the clubs certainly weren't going to help develop them with anything more sophisticated than tossing people in at the deep end and watching them sink or swim. That which didn't kill them supposedly made them stronger and the survivors often became long-term captains because, well, the clubs knew the process of changing captains was fraught with perils. I thought the clubs were looking through the wrong end of their binoculars. They saw players as liabilities to be managed rather than assets to be developed.

~

LIKE ALL THE OTHER AFL clubs, the game's ever-increasing profile meant St Kilda was receiving an increasing number of requests for players to attend events like school fetes or fundraisers for service organisations. The expectations weren't great, so long as the players turned up looking slightly embarrassed and signed a few autographs before quietly slinking away. I suggested to Stan that if we could offer the players some broader communication training they might be a bit more relaxed and forthcoming at these events, which would be good for all involved.

Some players were still working other jobs so there was no possibility of holding the sessions during the day and we scheduled them after football training, which meant that players who did attend would have to stay back at the club until nine or ten o'clock at night. There was no obligation for the players to attend the sessions but there was a good turnout nevertheless.

Like any practical skill, they weren't going to get better at public speaking by thinking about it or listening to someone else talk about it. They were encouraged to relate to the rest of the group a story about their days before arriving at St Kilda. Nothing complicated, just a recollection from their past. For example, Darryl Wakelin talked about his memories when his father was coaching at the local football club and he was in the land of giants, the team's mascot being tortured underneath an itchy old woollen jumper, the chewing gum he'd nicked from the trainers spilling out of his pockets as he ran onto the ground with the team before the game.

Hour after hour they went around the room and told story after story about themselves and one after another they grew more comfortable with the idea that they could actually do it. The exercise justified itself from a purely getting-to-know-one-another-better perspective but the benefits were more profound than that.

A few weeks into the training, I got word of a fundraiser that was going to be held in Horsham for a young man who'd suffered a brain injury on the football field. The organisers had received some donations from AFL clubs but what they really wanted was someone to speak at a fundraising breakfast.

I asked Darryl Wakelin and Rod Keogh if they would be prepared to come along with me. We'd go the night before, stay the night in Horsham, and at the breakfast they could try a bit of public speaking? They agreed and a few days later we headed west.

Darryl and Rod presented not as nervous, aloof AFL footballers but as genuine young country blokes who were keen to be there and keen to talk and very quickly they had the audience captivated. They told some stories about themselves, ran some auctions, drew the raffle and talked with anyone who'd talk with them. I could see how their skills had developed, and were continuing to develop as I watched on.

Towards the end of proceedings the injured boy's father got up to thank Darryl and Rod for their efforts but he broke down and couldn't go on. Mum came to Dad's rescue and tried to finish his speech but she broke down too. The club president stepped in and, while finding it very difficult, managed to get through the speech. We bid our farewells and drove back to Melbourne, not a word spoken in the car for a long time afterwards.

That breakfast has stayed with me. It told me that footballers' hallowed status in the community doesn't have to work to the detriment of the players' personal development. The situation can be made to work in everyone's favour. Such is the status of elite sportspeople in the community, they don't have to be heard, only seen, to have people eating out of their hands. How much good work could be done if the footballers brought along something that was a bit more substantial than their high profile? There'd be winners everywhere.

As I saw it, it was a matter of raising our expectations of sportspeople and then giving them the opportunity and the assistance required for them to meet those expectations. I wasn't sure how that would look in practice or what kind of structures would have to be in place to create some kind of athlete development agency that could address player development more formally, but there was a clearly a gap there worth bridging.

We were barely scratching the issue's surface at St Kilda and there were obviously massive benefits to be gained by developing the players into something more substantial than faces staring out of a cereal box. I was beginning to have florid visions of legions of athlete-facilitators fanning out to all corners of the community, delivering all kinds of positive messages. But that was also a confrontation with my own limitations as a sole trader. If there were ten of me, maybe I could begin to do something about it on a broader scale.

My business as a leadership and teamwork trainer carried one rather large and inescapable irony, if not an outright hypocrisy. There was only one of me. One man working alone. Lone Wolf Enterprises. Where was my team?

~

STAN ALVES ALSO SAW the many risks for young players with good incomes, only part-time demands from football in terms of hours required at the club and limited life skills to be able to cope with that mix of circumstances. The worst case scenarios were already occurring with some players habitually gambling or settling into lifestyles that revolved around sleeping in until they were due at training and spending their downtime watching video after video or playing electronic games.

If we could get the players to have some other focus outside their football, we theorised, and get them involved in something where they could develop some non-football skills and make a positive contribution to other people in the process, that would be beneficial to the individual, the team, the club and the community.

One of the best ways to learn skills is teaching them, so we figured that, rather than sitting players down together and hammering them about the importance of getting their lives into order, if we got them to teach life skills it would keep them gainfully occupied and they might learn some life skills along the way.

We looked around and decided to develop a life-skills program that the players could deliver to secondary schools. Phil Anstey, St Kilda's player development manager, did much of the leg work to get this program up and running. The program was delivered predominantly to Year 9 and 10 students and kids who were regarded as 'at risk'. We'd train up some players as facilitators and we'd concentrate on kids in the Dandenong–Frankston region, on the outer south-eastern fringes of Melbourne, in partnership with the Department of Justice. The program would be called 'Start Me Up'.

Facilitators need to develop not only questioning skills but an ability to engage people and build a rapport with them. That means being able to elaborate on their own experiences and identifying what they'd learned from those experiences. The stereotypical view of an AFL player is that they are lucky and that life must have fallen into place for them just like that, and it was important that kids knew that everyone had had setbacks at one time or another and had to deal with them.

To prepare the players—David Sierakowski, Robert Harvey, Tony Brown, Joel Smith, Austinn Jones, Matthew Lappin, Jason Cripps, Justin Peckett, Chris Hemley and Daniel Healey—we got them to think through their own personal experiences and to tell stories about them so they'd be armed with those recollections when they went out to work with kids. As we'd learned with the previous groups there were benefits all round from them standing in front of their peers and telling the group about the happiest day of their life, their biggest disappointment, their life goals and the steps they were taking to achieve that goal. Above all, it helped them better understand themselves.

The players were made familiar with the notion of experiential learning and how to garner feedback from the kids on how the sessions went. How well did you think the session worked? What worked and what didn't? How can we get better next time?

The sessions were an eye-opener for the players as they learned how young people and their situations can severely challenge beliefs and opinions and put a professional football career into its proper perspective. Football is hard, but not that hard when compared with the lives some of the kids were leading.

As the players helped the kids develop strategies for improving their situation, we noticed those players were beginning to take on board their own lessons. After a poor performance on the football field, they had a model to follow for working through their own performance issues. What worked? What didn't work? How can I improve? Without any doubt whatsoever, those players' match-day performances improved.

Maybe something else was happening that we couldn't see, or it was all purely coincidental? Whatever it was, the work they were doing certainly didn't seem to be doing the players any harm.

The life-skills program became a very powerful learning tool, for the kids and the players. The range of benefits to the players, of course, depended on how much effort they were putting into the program.

Players benefited for all sorts of reasons. For example, Robert Harvey indicated to me very early on in my involvement at St Kilda that one of his goals was to become a leader at the club. He was already an elite player and, while there has never been an issue with his character, his football abilities or his commitment to the team, he was one of the shyest people at the club and he accepted that for him to be a better team player he'd have to extend himself by developing his communication skills and be more comfortable giving feedback to his team-mates and challenging them to improve. His motive for taking on the training was clear and while it didn't turn him into an extrovert, the results were also clear. By challenging himself and becoming more forthcoming around the team he made a massive contribution to its improvement.

Another player, Justin Peckett, was on thin ice at St Kilda in 1995. He'd had a number of scrapes off the field and there were some lifestyle concerns. The match committee were in serious discussions about whether to keep Justin in the system. At the same time, Justin was getting involved in 'Start Me Up'.

Through the facilitation and learning process and working with other people, Justin began to understand himself much better and made some changes. Ten years later he's played over two hundred games for St Kilda, is the club's second-longest serving current player after Robert Harvey, and has gone on to be an excellent facilitator who can work with a variety of groups.

St Kilda had a marginally better year in 1996 in terms of match results. The team won the pre-season competition, the Ansett Cup as it was known, with a new crop of young players in the side. Expectations were raised on the grounds that a pre-season 'premiership' has often been the precursor to a day premiership. There's no particular correlation between the two, other than a couple of sides have done it.

During 1996, in the wake of their pre-season success, the players expectations of one another certainly increased and the team began to show genuine signs of improvement. In the end though, the team lost more games than it won during the home-and-away season, fell a couple of victories short of the finals and finished in tenth position.

~

I WAS STILL HEADING over the border to keep up with Central District and monitor their progress. They'd managed to make the 1996 finals, their fourth successive finals appearance, and again they made it through to the grand final. They fronted up against Port Adelaide again, and once again fell short.

If there was a pattern over there of losing grand finals—and two of anything in a row is regarded as a pattern in some circles— it was definitely a preferable pattern to sitting down the bottom watching other teams lose grand finals. We did some work with the players to make sure they understood there's no such thing as a jinx unless they believe there is, and to encourage them to stick with their program. They weren't doing a lot wrong and if they could cut through the disappointment and continue to learn from their losses it was only a matter of time before they broke through and won the big one.

The approach we'd taken at Centrals wasn't about rising out of the ashes, pinching a flag and falling away again, it was about maintaining the values and structures and personnel that would give the club its best chance of maintaining a consistent high standard of performance, something that cannot be judged on the outcome of one particular football match. It's a simple equation— if you're up there often enough you'll win your fair share. If losing two out of two grand finals wasn't a fair share, they only had to stick to their guns and the tide would turn for them. If they hadn't won a flag yet, they'd certainly won the respect of their competition and that, for the club and the team, was a major turnaround.

The other big news over in Adelaide was Port Adelaide's admission to the AFL for the 1997 season. Port needed as many good football people on board as they could find and one of them was Alan Stewart, who became Port Adelaide's National Recruiting Manager.

ARRESTED DEVELOPMENT

St Kilda continued to improve through 1997 and finished the home-and-away season sitting atop the premiership ladder. They did well over the next month, comfortably winning two finals and making it through to the grand final, the club's first appearance there since 1971. As it happened, the North Ballarat Rebels also made it through to the grand final that year so it was a fairly big day out for me, with the Rebels on the MCG in the morning and the Saints in the afternoon. It was more evidence to me that even if the framework wasn't doing teams much good, it certainly wasn't hurting them. The Rebels won, the Saints lost.

The AFL is so fiercely competitive that an incremental improvement or decline in performance can make a profound but nevertheless disproportionate difference to not only the team's ladder position but also the club's view of itself. The ladder, like the scoreboard, is nothing more than an historical marker of how you've been going. It doesn't tell you anything about tomorrow.

Stan persevered with the framework at St Kilda through 1998 but the club learned little from its previous failures, or its successes, and after the grand final defeat the whispers and innuendo were back, suggesting that if not for certain mistakes by certain people at certain times the club would most certainly have its second premiership cup in the foyer. The recriminations were underway, just like the St Kilda of old.

The team had changed its ways but the club was much more resistant. When the team won eleven of the first fourteen games of 1998 and sat on top of the ladder the club saw no need whatsoever to arrest the corrosive talk around the club—the club, not the team—about alternative coaches who surely would have done better with such a super team and won the previous season's grand final.

I voiced my concerns to the administration and was dealt with succinctly: 'Haven't you seen where we are on the ladder? What's the problem?'

History says that in 1998 St Kilda lost six of its last eight home-and-away matches, just scraped into the finals, lost both finals matches and Stan was sacked at the end of the season.

A lot has been said and written about 'player power' having been responsible for Stan's demise, about how he lost the support of the playing group and how the club responded to that. I don't subscribe to that theory. I believe the players were 'informally' asked questions about Stan's performance. The players answered honestly, having every reason to believe that the rules they'd grown accustomed to about delivering feedback and how it would be used would still apply.

That chain of events indicated to me that, firstly, we'd made significant inroads with the playing group in terms of their honesty with each other and their ability to manage their own team based around their trademark and behaviours. And, secondly, that the message hadn't spread far beyond the playing group. Following Stan's dismissal, my decision to leave St Kilda wasn't a difficult one as the club's actions were so contrary to the principles we'd been developing that staying on wasn't an option.

Unsurprisingly, the next coach, former Essendon champion, Tim Watson, was unable to get anything out of the team— memorably describing his coaching experience as a time when he slept like a baby because he woke up bawling every couple of hours—and after two seasons he moved on.

The Saints then moved heaven and earth to get Malcolm Blight out of retirement to work some miracles for them, briefly presenting a united front by sending delegations of administrators and cap-in-hand players to see him, and refusing to take no for an answer. Malcolm relented and took on the team but no miracles were immediately forthcoming, and shortly after he mentioned to the media midway through his very first season that the St Kilda culture was 'five hundred per cent worse than at any other club he's seen', he was sacked.

Under Stan Alves the club managed a grand final appearance in 1997 and another finals appearance in 1998. In the four seasons after Stan's dismissal the team finished tenth, sixteenth, fifteenth and fifteenth.

Working with St Kilda was a extraordinary opportunity for me to implement and evaluate the framework at sport's elite level, as well as presenting me with a number of opportunities to work with other sports clubs and businesses. I'll be forever grateful to Stan Alves and the club for taking the risk because at the time human resource management was largely non-existent in football and most clubs were firmly convinced that the only way to improve their team's performance was to recruit better players. The idea that the best footballers in the land still had a lot to learn about football and life might well have been widely known back then but the reality was that very little was being done about it. During his coaching stint at St Kilda, Stan Alves changed that situation and, hopefully, forever.

~

Following Stan's departure, the then Collingwood coach, Tony Shaw, contacted me and indicated he was keen on implementing the program at his club, which we did. We did the groundwork as we had at Centrals and St Kilda and found similar discrepancies between what the players were saying and what they were doing.

We progressed quickly to the peer evaluation stage, where the players were rated according to the team's values and behaviours, and it went well until we got to one of the more senior players. Looking on, it was obvious the players were struggling to deliver their feedback. They went round in circles, over here and over there and never quite getting to the point. Eventually one of the younger players stood up and apologised to the senior player for not having been more honest in the past and then proceeded to appraise his work ethic and propensity for taking short cuts. At the same time the young player was clearly challenging the other players as well, as if to ask why, after the senior player had been at the club so long, was it only now that he was hearing this? That led to a broader discussion about why that feedback had not been delivered long before it had. As the senior player learned, it was because, in essence, they were afraid of his reaction.

Peer evaluation isn't a blood sport but if the feedback doesn't address the most pressing issues about the player's behaviours that need to improve then, obviously, that player and the team certainly won't improve as much as they would otherwise.

~

AT THE END OF THAT FIRST YEAR at Collingwood, Tony Shaw stood down and Mick Malthouse was appointed as senior coach. Mick made it clear to me very early on that he hadn't had anyone work with him in this area before but he was prepared to run with the framework and see how it went.

In preparation for the 2000 season the Collingwood leadership group headed to Ballarat for a two-day workshop where they received some facilitation training and some tips on how they could run their own workshops. Shortly afterwards the leadership group took the rest of the team to Ballarat for a two-day planning workshop where they decided on what kind of team they wanted to be, the behaviours that must underpin that team, and to review the positions in the leadership group. At the end of the workshop they returned to Melbourne and presented the outcomes to the coaches.

There was a great deal of scepticism about the exercise outside of the playing group. Few were prepared to believe that footballers were capable of going away on their own without the coaches or other staff being involved and spend their time productively. But that, unfortunately, is the widespread perception of footballers, as people who aren't smart or disciplined or responsible enough to look after their own best interests. But the Ballarat workshops were, I believe, a potent learning experience for the players and I'd like to think that those involved would agree that the trademarks they developed at the workshops helped sustain them over the next couple of seasons that included successive grand final appearances in 2002 and 2003.

The open feedback process certainly caused some tensions at Collingwood. While Mick Malthouse actively used and encouraged the leadership group he seemed less interested in using the team's trademark to guide decisions made around the club.

The coaching staff were anxious from the outset about what would happen if a good player received negative feedback. When that happened, the feedback process was immediately watered down.

My view, of course, was that we would manage any fallout. And if it turned out that any player was so unwilling or incapable of hearing out their team-mates feedback then it was self-evident that the player wouldn't be much good to that team in the long run anyway. But if the management has reservations about the process and there's an unwillingness to follow through to logical conclusions, which is when the real benefits of the framework kick in, it's better not to engage in the process at all.

To use the framework successfully, managers and coaches have to at the very least be seen to support the team's trademark and be willing to follow through on the hard calls it invariably sends their way. Otherwise, the piece of paper that says this team values X over Y becomes just that, a piece of paper that's worse than useless as it's just adding to the confusion. When doubts have crept into a team about what's really going to be rewarded it becomes a steep uphill battle maintaining let alone improving performance

Following Malcolm Blight's mid-season dismissal from St Kilda in 2001 a revamped board of directors appointed Grant Thomas to the job. I met with Grant and the club's new president, Rod Butterss. They said they felt there would be benefits to my coming back to St Kilda and re-establishing the program there.

Grant Thomas has a different background to the vast majority of AFL coaches. He came in with a very strong business background and had implemented similar initiatives with teams he'd coached prior to the Saints. He was very much in favour of a leadership group selected by its peers and having clear trademark behaviours in place. He applied that philosophy to his football department and set up the coaching team under a similar framework and conducted peer reviews. That indicated to me that the implementation and development of the framework wouldn't be so difficult because I wouldn't be trying to sell the concept so much as assisting someone who genuinely wanted it in place.

Grant was keen to have someone in a full-time role, managing peer evaluations and managing the young players' development. The latter idea, of having the young players in their own discrete 'leadership' group and concentrating on their development, seemed, to me, like a terrific idea. They could meet separately and focus themselves on their own performance and training objectives and, hopefully, accelerate their development as leaders. That young group included people like Nick Riewoldt, Justin Koschitzke, Luke Ball, Nick Del Santo and Matt McGuire, players who were going to be St Kilda's future.

Separating the young players from the group might seem an odd way to build a team but when we tried to mix up the young players with the older players previously, we found the juniors would defer to the more experienced players and allow them to lead while they followed and no one was learning much from it.

Soon after the group was established a couple of senior players came to me and asked about what was going on with the young blokes. Their enthusiasm was having an impact on training.

We conducted separate, extended exercises for the young players, sometimes over a three- or four-day period, where the players were given a limited amount of information about the tasks they'd be undertaking and there was a strong focus on activities requiring initiative. The tasks were physically demanding so decision-making and leadership skills could be tested when they were fatigued.

One four-day exercise in the Grampians involved a series of lengthy navigation tasks that would, with some good decisions, return a group to where they'd begun from. A group I was following got lost; as a facilitator, I wouldn't intervene unless the situation became unsafe and I could see where we were on the map and knew they weren't heading into a dire situation. So I was just following along behind the group and monitoring where they were on the map as they headed a long way off course. Eventually they stopped for a drink and I asked them how they thought it was going.

'I think we're lost.'

That led to a discussion: 'How long do you think you've been lost?'

One said 'I haven't known where we've been since we left the car park.'

Another chimed in: 'I haven't been sure for maybe the last half-hour.'

No one could put their finger on the map and say, 'This is where we are now.' They were all lost. And by not saying anything, they were a lot further off course than they might have been if someone had piped up earlier. We related that back to football and what a similar situation might be on the field. It was, one of them said, like losing football matches and having no other solution but continuing to try harder. You've lost all sense of team, and you don't say anything to anyone else because you're not sure yourself. So you try harder, on your own.

We discussed it further. What do we do? One of the boys made an extraordinarily sage-like observation, although I'm not sure he understood the profound nature of it because he delivered it as a joke. He said, 'Get us a senior player ... Nathan Burke wouldn't walk for two hours lost, he'd stop everyone and then do something about it ...'

And that was the point of the exercise. This was the key to their development. If the club was going to succeed, these young players had to be like Nathan Burke or Robert Harvey or Stuart

Loewe. They would have to use their own judgment and if they couldn't see the sense in what they were doing they had to be confident enough to call a halt to proceedings until they were satisfied. They mustn't just go along with situations they weren't sure about and they had to trust themselves.

Grant decided he wanted to run with a rotating captaincy to accelerate learning. Instead of the usual captaincy criteria of seniority or football ability, the young players in the leadership group would take the reins for a period of time before passing the job on to the next person. For all the cynicism and negativity that initiative met in the media I have no doubt that in the future people will see the arrangement for what it really is, which is a tool for accelerating the development of leadership in a club.

The rotating captaincy has several positives and, as far as I can tell, no negatives. A young player can rightfully aspire to be a leader of the club and the evidence is that the captaincy experience does help the development of leaders. Robert Harvey improved as a leader when he was captain and continues to show that leadership around the club. Aaron Hamill improved dramatically as a leader during his time as captain but his leadership didn't drop off when the next player took over the role. The next in line, Lenny Hayes, improved as a leader dramatically during his time as captain, as did Nick Riewoldt and Luke Ball, and so it goes on.

THE ATHLETES EMERGE

AUSTRALIAN FOOTBALL LEAGUE CLUBS can be like parallel universes and we didn't realise while we were setting up the 'Start Me Up' program at St Kilda that ten or so kilometres away at the Melbourne Football Club a similar program was being established. Their version was called 'Life's a Ball', co-ordinated by someone called Gerard Murphy in partnership with 'Here For Life', its focus on youth suicide. Gerard Murphy? The student-teacher at Donald High School? He'd left teaching and was the communications manager at Melbourne Football Club.

Here for Life wanted to expand the Life's a Ball program nationally using six to eight players from each AFL club to deliver their message. Gerard left his job with the football club to take up the role with Here For Life and he approached me to train the athletes as facilitators.

Life's a Ball became increasingly successful. Schools were reporting positive outcomes, clubs were seeing improved self-management skills and, above all from their perspective, improved match-day performances from the players, and we were seeing some highly effective facilitators emerging. There was something in this.

Gerard and I noticed that the charities' focus, not unreasonably, was the delivery of the program and its message. But if the athletes were going to commit to the hard yards of learning all the skills required to take groups through any kind of meaningful program, there not only had to be work for them to do, there had to be more structure in it for the players than endless sessional work. We believed that if someone was to focus on the athletes and their development outcomes, these facilitators could deliver a range of programs in a variety of environments; for example, schools, workplaces, jails, and other elite sporting teams and, potentially, work with us full-time at the ends of their athletic careers. If Leading Teams came into existence at any particular moment, it was then.

Here we go again, I thought. Sally and I had just spent around eight or nine years establishing a comfortable single-seater training business of our own and here we were, going straight back into a risk-taking phase like when I first left the air force. For Gerard it was a similar story; high-risk and a strong argument (by his soon-to-be wife, Liz) that this was not great timing.

There were a couple of big questions hanging over the idea and most of those revolved around explaining its benefits. It was one thing to be able to see them, another to put something down on paper that gave people a rough idea of what we were talking about. It could easily read like a pitch for another snake oil remedy, the athletes coming across as a gimmick we were using to sell a product. There was plenty of that around, with all sorts of prominent sportspeople somehow growing new hair or losing fifty kilos by starting the day with Brand X muesli. It couldn't be anything like that. The athletes would have to bring real people skills along with them, and from the athlete's point of view the work would have to lead somewhere worth their going to.

The other key questions were whether elite sports organisations would see it as being in their own interests to sponsor their own athletes' development into facilitators, whether our corporate customers could see athletes as valid facilitators in a business environment, whether other sports clubs and community organisations would see it as being worthwhile receiving the kind of leadership and teamwork training the Performance Improvement Program offered them, and if any of the above were so, would we be able to generate the significant funds that would be required to train the athletes to deliver the programs anyway?

There was little value in approaching sporting organisations with 'do the right thing' arguments because, as I'd learned, they get a lot of letters. They had to be able to understand that it was in their own interests to invest in their athletes and that the dividends would be evident out there on the park. If the bean counters were going to be moved they had to see how the investment could help the team win more games and thereby improve the balance sheet.

We would offer a part-time job to athletes that they could be developing skills in while their main focus was on a professional sporting career, with the possibility of the part-time work then leading to a career after sport. Facilitating leadership and team development programs doesn't appeal to everyone—many, actually—as a career choice, but it would present as a fantastic opportunity to some others. We would concentrate on those with the highest aptitude and strongest motivation for the work.

The one problem we faced was that I needed to train athletes but also generate income as a facilitator. I called on Kraig Grime, my ex-air force colleague, and explained the situation. Kraig had left the RAAF some years earlier and he was working in a training business of his own. Beyond his training skills, his management and business background would be a huge advantage to us. He agreed to help, and he stepped in like he had when I was bumbling through leadership training at Point Cook and steered us through mazes of procedures and paperwork and got us organised.

What would the business look like? It would be growing three separate arms. One would be continuing the kind of work we'd already been doing with athletes by training them up and plugging them into community programs. We would continue to develop the Performance Improvement Program and its related leadership programs and team development programs in the elite sports environment. And, thirdly, we would continue to deliver to corporate teams that same PIP model we'd been delivering to the sports teams adapted to the business environment. If it came off, we were going to be busy.

Our business discussions necessarily involved Kraig reducing commercial concepts to something we could understand, and eventually we ended up with a business structure. For a while there we called ourselves 'Athlete Development Australia', which might have been all right if our focus was exclusively on developing athletes. We eventually settled on 'Leading Teams'.

The idea of working in a team again was, I'll confess, a little daunting. I'd managed to get through the RAAF years running largely my own race and I had to think back to Donald High School to recall myself functioning in a workplace team and there wasn't a lot to console myself with there; that was a very good team and I was one of the weaker links to begin with and grew weaker as time went by. So I wasn't exactly bristling with confidence that I could pull my weight this time around and the fallout would be far worse if I failed to come through.

But there were grounds for optimism, I thought, because I'd dealt with plenty of people who were uncertain of their role in a team and how best to do their job and if I'd been able to help them sort it out I should be able to sort it out for myself. Obviously the new business ought to be adopting the leadership and teamwork model I'd been advocating to my clients for no other reason than it would seem very odd if we didn't, but beyond that imperative it was an elegant solution to a number of issues. It dealt with my only real misgiving about the venture, which was whether I could learn to be a team player and fit into a business structure. Plus, running the business using the principles I'd been advocating meant we'd develop a better appreciation of what our clients face when we front up at their workplaces with rolls of butchers' paper tucked under our arms. The business would be a working model of our own philosophies, one we could observe in operation from the inside, and those insights would be helpful when we were taking the model to other businesses and groups. If we went down in flames because we couldn't make the performance improvement model work in our situation it'd be a fine Darwinian conclusion to the idea.

I'd outlined the framework so many times to other people it was second nature to me but I still did a double-take when I thought about what it would look like. How did it go again? We'd decide on what kind of team we wanted to be and how we wanted to be seen and work from there. Our decision-making thereafter would be guided by those values we'd all signed off on. We'd hold regular feedback and peer review sessions where our behaviour would be related to our trademark. We'd strive for constant improvement and everyone would know exactly where they stood with everyone else as we tried for 'systematic honesty'.

~

THERE'S PROBABLY a couple of books in Jason Cripps's story but he'll have to write them himself. Jason arrived at St Kilda via its supplementary list, which was for players who are not on the team roster but can be selected in an emergency. Jason managed to win the reserves best-and-fairest award while on the supplementary list and then got his lifeline to senior football when a listed player grew weary of the game and surrendered his spot.

Shortly after establishing himself as an AFL player Jason suffered a dreadful leg injury when his right hamstring detached itself from the bone, a rare and unusual situation even for Australian football which is notorious for testing out the 'hammies'. At one stage he was confined to bed for four months, unable to move. The medical advice said his career was over but he learned to walk again and dealt with the psychological issues the situation had raised, and after three years of intensive rehabilitation resumed his journey in the AFL.

Jason is an outstanding example of someone who'd copped all the knock-backs and setbacks and had been resilient enough to have kept pursuing their dreams. His goals were so far away they were over the horizon but he identified them, worked towards them and ultimately achieved them.

As Jason made his way back into the game he was delivering a life-skills programs to 'at risk' kids and I believe that may have helped him deal with the enormous setbacks he'd suffered and provided some necessary perspective and detachment that's too often missing from the world of professional sport where a missed shot or a dropped catch can register as a 'tragedy'.

We arranged with the Department of Justice to run a four-part goal-setting program in Victorian prisons and youth training centres. This was somewhat more challenging than working in schools—if that's not too much of an understatement—and the players who conducted those sessions were forced by necessity to develop their skill levels dramatically.

The reality of facilitator training is that you cannot cover every contingency and trainee facilitators are put into environments where the questions they'll be asked and the challenges issued are out of everyone's control. All you can do is try to build the facilitator's skill base so they might cope.

One day we'd been discussing with some prisoners their dreams and goals and looking at strategies the inmates could use to make them a reality. Some prisoners had indicated that for them the best bet was to get a job and try to dissociate themselves from the relationships outside that kept them in the crime cycle. Some others suggested they need to be better parents and it's hard to be a good parent when you're in jail, so focusing on their kids' welfare might help keep them going straight.

Jason Cripps asked a young prisoner about his goals. The boy answered through clenched teeth: 'My goal? Vengeance.'

Aside from my concerns for the lad, I was deeply concerned for Jason. The very last thing anyone needed was a group of prisoners drilling down into the topic of vengeance to see how they felt about it. A knee-jerk response might have been to dismiss the lad's reply and get back onto safer ground as soon as humanly possible. But denying the boy's feelings would probably achieve the opposite effect, leaving him angry and frustrated. It would be up to Jason to defuse the situation and it could go either way. I moved a little closer to the door.

Jason heard him out. Then, rather than directly addressing the topic of revenge, Jason talked about the concept of choices and consequences. He related his life experience and talked about it in terms of choices and consequences, and how the life we lead here and now is a consequence of those choices we'd made earlier. The ball was in our court, no one else's. He engaged the prisoner without confronting him and the group had a productive discussion thereafter about the personal costs of having revenge as a goal. Jason handled it as well as any human services professional could have and afterwards I had to remind myself that he was actually a footballer by trade.

Jason became the football development manager at St Kilda, working with the young players much as I did when I began at the club in 1994, and has now moved into coaching roles.

~

TRENT HOTTON'S chequered early history as an AFL player preceded him. Collingwood unceremoniously dumped him for some off-field misdemeanours and he could easily have thrown in the proverbial towel. He didn't. He went back to suburban football, stayed fit and continued to study at university and proved unequivocally to anyone who was still watching him that he could get his life back on track. He coped admirably with life in the shadow of the Legend of Trent Hotton, which must have been more testing than dealing with the relatively simple lifestyle issues that had initially brought him undone.

No sooner had Trent proven that he wasn't dependent on football and was going to be successful on his own terms, he got another opportunity at the AFL level and thereafter played three seasons with Carlton. He began working as a facilitator during that time and it was obvious that he was an outstanding prospect as we sent him off to the most demanding kinds of sessions knowing that he would not just survive, he'd handle them with style.

Anyone who has heard a good public speaker has felt the sense of being uplifted by the person's words. But translating that motivation, or inspiration, or whatever it is, into long-term sustainable performance improvements can be a tricky proposition. It's all right to have every nerve ending tingling and synapses going off like fireworks but what next? What do you do now to make good use of all that energy? Stand there punching the air for the rest of the day?

In reality, Trent would only have to stand up and tell his story of how he overcame adversity, and he could easily make a living doing just that, firing people up to punch more air more often. The crowds could then disperse knowing that if they were ever sacked in public and labelled by the media as a very naughty boy, they'd have a good idea of the steps required to redeem their situation.

But you'd have to be one very inspired accounts clerk to be able to work out how to apply Trent or anyone else's personal story to your job. Yet that's the clear expectation many businesses and other organisations have when they bring in external people to motivate or inspire their staff to new heights. We often see successful athletes paraded around for one-off motivational sessions or whatever. As a goodwill or feel-good gesture, that's fine, but to actually link one-off sessions to performance improvements, as some do, is stretching the boundaries somewhat.

People who turned up to Trent's sessions expecting to hear a string of colourful stories were surprised. People warmed to him because here was someone who hadn't led a perfect life but had very obviously picked himself up, dusted himself down and got on with it. And while they'd certainly learn a lot about Trent's situation, they'd learn infinitely more about themselves and how to apply the performance improvement model at a team or individual level.

Every facilitator is different, with their own particular style and emphases and it was evident that Trent had a very practical take on situations and, being a very good listener, was able to relate his lessons to other people's circumstances. His groups went away with a very strong idea about exactly what they had to do next. As did Gerard, Kraig and I when after three seasons Carlton dropped Trent into the dumpster. We appointed him to our staff, where he joined former elite heptathlete, Belinda Jakiel, as our first full-time athlete facilitators.

~

EVERYONE WHO UNDERWENT a Performance Improvement Program, whether they were in a sports or sales team or a community group, were asked for feedback about what had worked for them, what hadn't, and where they thought we could do better in the future. With constant adjustments and fine tuning the program evolved from one month to the next. Sometimes we introduced what we thought were improvements only to learn from the feedback that we'd actually gone backwards. Other times a slight change to an exercise proved to be a great leap forward.

As one team after another adopted the principles and put them into practice it was clear that some exercises were more effective than others in certain environments. Subtle patterns began to emerge in the way teams responded and we were beginning to be able to identify for ourselves what the key learning moments in the program were. Before too long we were able to edit the program back to its most effective components and deliver those in shorter timeframes, which was a good thing too because the more we explored what kind of environment individuals required to deliver optimal performance, the more information there was to deliver.

Eventually, after years of constant tweaking, the program began to solidify into its current form, which is a behaviour-based decision-making framework for managing the entire lifecycle of any given team, from a member's induction to their eventual retirement from the team.

These days we have a set of criteria we can refer to in assessing whether the program is likely to be able assist a particular organisation. The program doesn't suit those seeking a miracle cure as it's hard work and very challenging for everyone involved, although, unlike a miracle cure, it does offer a fighting chance of long-term success.

As we'd seen with sports teams, it simply isn't satisfactory to have a team go about things differently while the remainder of the organisation continues on as it always had. For the program to be successful it is essential for the senior management to buy into the process and identify with the trademark and the behaviours the team has agreed upon. Nowadays we won't even start on a Performance Improvement Program with an organisation if its senior management is unwilling to buy into the process.

Taking Care of Business

OUR FIRST MAJOR CORPORATE engagement got underway in 1998 when I was asked to establish a 'Future Leaders program' at Monash University's Caulfield campus on behalf on the student union. Andrew O'Brien was its general manager at the time.

The university then merged all its support services under the one umbrella and Andrew was appointed Chief Executive Officer of Monyx, the new university service organisation. Andrew believed in our program's principles and applied them to the senior management team, and then throughout the entire organisation. In the early days of the program's implementation he met all sorts of resistance to such a radical idea, much of which will be detailed in his own book, I'm sure. He was resilient enough to persevere until the weight of numbers was on his side. The program is now firmly in place and been successful enough to have been evaluated and then adopted by other universities.

Some years ago we began working in New South Wales with a team of forty people in the finance industry where we met the classic 'gap' between the company's deeply impressive values and mission statement and the group's behaviour. As became evident, there was no sense of ownership by staff of those values, they were just some more words in a sea of words.

We went through the process: how they thought they were perceived, how they wanted to be perceived and what kind of behaviours that needed to be in place to generate that perception. As always, the challenge for them was being frank enough with one another to expose the behaviours that were being tolerated in their workplace that were counterproductive.

As we worked our way through those issues, we also looked at who were the real leaders in their workplace; that is, who were the closest to modelling the behaviours that the team said they aspired to, and who would have the courage to challenge others if they saw others in breach of agreed behaviours?

Asking who the real leaders are in a business environment can produce as many surprises as it does with sports teams because, like the sports teams, there is often very little correlation between position or seniority and behaviours.

Nor, it has to be said, is there any great correlation between longevity with an organisation and loyalty. It simply cannot be assumed that because someone has been with an organisation since before time began they are any more loyal to the organisation than someone who only just arrived. It simply doesn't work that way. Loyalty to the team or firm can and hopefully will translate into longevity, but long service can occur simply because nothing happened to prevent it; the person has never left of their own volition and they've never been forced to. But beyond that, it's an open question as to why they are still there after so many years. Is it loyalty or inertia? Dedication to their job or a comfort zone? Is there a willingness there to commit to the team's goals or not?

There's no simple answer, yet I've seen managers who will only ever go one of two ways. Either they simply *never* tackle their most senior staff, or their modus operandi is to go in with extreme prejudice and get rid of the most senior personnel on the grounds that it simply has to be done before they can effect culture change. Decisions get made but they aren't based on relevant information or around any agreed framework. It's a far less complicated call when a person's behaviour is set against the team's espoused behaviours, and far more likely to result in something approaching justice not only being done but, as importantly, being seen to be done by the rest of the team.

Reminiscent of what I'd seen with overtly talented footballers, I worked with an organisation that was effectively being held to ransom by an engineer who was the only staff member familiar with a particular system. He was using his specialist knowledge like a barrel to hold people over, the general theme being that the business needed him more than it needed the other staff members and that, to him, translated as being able to take more liberties than other staff members. He'd got away with it for so long it seemed to have reinforced in his mind that it was okay to behave as he was, which was proudly uncommunicative, intransigent, impatient and impulsive.

We embarked on the process and it became painfully apparent that he wasn't going to participate in any kind of team development because he didn't see himself as one of the team. His team was beneath him. The senior management were so inured to his attitude they barely batted an eyelid: Why would he participate in team-building sessions? He never participates. He's the Chief Engineer.

They'd baulked at doing something about his behaviour so often that it had ceased to be even raised as an issue at management meetings and, as if the engineer were a malfunctioning computer, they devised a set of workarounds to avoid having to tackle him. His behaviour cast a shadow over all of their activities but because it was in the too-hard basket they kept themselves busy addressing all kinds of lesser issues as if those would make the difference. Now, years later, the chief engineer's behaviour was no longer seen by them as an impediment to improved performance because, in effect, they no longer saw him at all. Paradoxically, the bigger and curlier the problem is, the more likely it is that we'll find reasons not to tackle it.

All right, so the engineer had a key role to play in the firm's day-to-day operation. But the narrow view he had of his role was negatively affecting his colleagues and effectively denying them any opportunity to improve their performance as a team. Either the engineer changed, they changed the engineer, or nothing changed.

Once the management accepted that it was inevitable that one day, sooner or later, they'd have to go through the awkward process of replacing him, their choices became clearer. They could fold their arms and wait or they could trust themselves to manage the scenario they'd feared for so long of having no one on hand to maintain their machinery. With some encouragement they opted for sooner rather than later and the engineer was sent on his way.

Having made that hard decision, a junior engineer was retrained in very short time—the job wasn't as specialised or complicated as the previous occupant had led them to believe—and not a minute of production was lost, which was a bonus because the real point of the exercise was restoring some congruency to the situation and sending a clear message to the team about what kind of behaviour would be rewarded and, above all, that the team's behaviours would ultimately prevail over other all other considerations, even something so crucial as risks to production.

As I'd witnessed with sporting teams, the act of following through on the hard calls sends such a powerful message —that no one, irrespective of status or position, can live outside the boundaries the team agreed upon—that the team's response will usually soften whatever blow is being expected.

When someone hasn't been pulling their weight and playing their role in the team, their departure is like pulling your hand from a bucket of water—it leaves a hole, but not for long. Like the football team minus their superstar, it was only after the new chief engineer settled into the role that the overall negative impact of the previous incumbent could be fully appreciated. Their team behaviours intact, the entire organisation took some giant steps forward with their new chief engineer at the heart of the action, which is where, they learned, their chief engineer needed to be all along. But if the team hadn't taken ownership of those behaviours and couldn't identify with the reasons behind the decision, there would have been a vastly different response.

The capacity in some workplaces for overlooking the obvious can be astounding. I worked with one group for many months, their discussions seemingly fixated on 'honesty' but without ever getting to the crux of the issue. One day, outside of the sessions, I was told there'd been thefts and pilfering going on there for decades. They knew who the culprit was: an otherwise kindly fellow who'd been there longer than most. Just about the first piece of information any of had them received at induction was to watch their valuables around this gentleman. The situation was too awkward for anyone to want to tackle him.

I once asked a business team about what sort of behaviours would they not tolerate in the workplace and a number of them said 'bullying'; more of them, in fact, than I would have expected. I said I was sensing that maybe there was some bullying going on in their workplace. And if it was happening, that meant it was actually being tolerated. What was going on? Nothing, apparently. *Everything* was fine. So we continued on, going through the motions. There was only one person who could rescue us and that would be someone who was prepared to be honest.

Right on cue the most recent arrival to the firm, a young kid in probably his first job, said 'People treat one another like dogs around here …' As it transpired, there was some bully in all of them. For all their HR manuals' acclamations about bullying being unacceptable and their own stated distaste for it, that was how things had traditionally got done around there. It went back a long way, several generations, and as one staff member after another came and went the behaviour was learned and then accepted.

~

OFTEN A TEAM WILL SAY it's going to adopt some core behaviours that will help the team be the kind of team it wants to be by, say, treating the customers with respect and listening to their needs. But how can that be if all management monitors is the amount of sales that the individuals within the team makes? Obviously there is going to be a conflict in the team members' minds. And particularly so if the managers have promoted people through the organisation based purely on their capacities in, say, a sales environment; it's only fair for the team to assume that in this workplace sales figures translate into your chances of promotion, not by how you treat the customers.

What is really being rewarded here? That's what everyone not only wants to know but has to know if they are going to survive. It's human nature to be looking at other people's behaviour and their situations and trying to nut out, in terms of getting rewards, what seems to be working and what doesn't.

A business might have a beautifully written document, and they often do, that tells staff all about the behaviours it espouses. But the glossy paper and the public relations consultant's language counts for precious little because people's behaviour is guided far less by what they read than by other people's behaviour as they observe it. We can't tell what anyone else is thinking, all we can do is watch what they do and see what happens next. Without there being rewards on offer for serving customers with extra care and attention, there can be no argument about it; customer service is not valued around here. If it were, then surely someone would be measuring it and rewarding it accordingly.

As with the sports teams we've worked with, a behaviours-based decision-making framework can require some new and different measurements of performance that are congruent with the team's values. For businesses, those can be derived from peer evaluations, as well as gathering feedback from customers or suppliers. But if the team's espoused behaviours aren't measured, supported and promoted above all other considerations, then, simply, they aren't the team's behaviours. And if the team isn't operating according to its own behaviours, the organisation the team represents will just have to accept that its staff, as a team, are operating well below par.

THREE-POINTERS, CONVERSIONS AND LONG SHOTS

IN MY FIRST YEAR AT COLLINGWOOD Football Club, the then coach of the Victorian Titans in the National Basketball League, Brian Goorjian, asked if he could come along and see what we were doing in the player development area. I got the Collingwood players' permission for Brian to sit in on a peer review session.

Brian was, perhaps, a little bit shocked by what he'd witnessed. He said afterwards that he felt his team was a long way from being able to cope with that kind of interpersonal intensity and that the basketball culture in general might not be ready for it. Or anyone that he could think of. We joked about me doing some work for him one day in the very distant future.

Four years later Brian had taken over as the coach of the Australian national basketball, the Boomers, and he wanted some team-building help.

The Boomers were a bit shaken. The starting line-up from the previous Olympics—Andrew Gaze, Luc Longley, Andrew Vlahov, Mark Bradtke and Shane Heal—had all retired from international duties around the same time and the team was beaten in the World Championship qualifiers by New Zealand and Brian had replaced the coach for that campaign, Phil Smyth.

Brian was left to choose his squad from twenty-five players who were unsure about where they fitted into the team, if at all, and there were some well-expressed doubts from basketball aficionados about the Boomers' ability to be competitive on the international stage any time soon given the team's apparent state of disarray.

In June 2002 we headed off to the Gold Coast for the first Boomers training camp with Brian as head coach. At the time the Victorian Titans franchise was undergoing some upheavals as the National Basketball League rationalised its situation in Melbourne and the Titans were absorbed into the Victorian Giants franchise. While on the camp Brian heard he wouldn't be the coach of the Giants, putting him in the unusual situation of being the national team's coach while not having a coaching role in the NBL.

That obviously wouldn't last long given Brian's coaching CV and soon afterwards, when Brett Brown, coach of the Sydney Kings, accepted an offer to take up an assistant coach's role in the United States with San Antonio Spurs in the National Basketball Association, Brian stepped in as the Kings' coach.

Like any other team embarking on the program, the Boomers began with an honest appraisal. Where do you think we are at? How do you think opposition view us? They said that there would be doubts about them and they'd probably be viewed as a 'moderate' team. When asked how they would like to be viewed, gold medals didn't feature. Like Centrals, St Kilda and Collingwood, they were more concerned about the deeper image of their team. They wanted to be seen as a tenacious, focused, professional and feared outfit. Their view was that they wanted every team that they played to walk off the court thinking that if they had a choice they would not want to play the Aussies again.

We then listed the sorts of behaviours that would be required to live their trademark or vision. This led us to a wide range of strategies in terms of their physical fitness, their hardness on court and how we would measure it, their behaviour off the court, and the sorts of steps that would be required for them to live up to their standards. They then went to China and competed very favourably in a world-class competition.

They came back to a camp at Gosford. We reviewed where we were at that point and all of the positive things that had been achieved in the previous tour. They then went off to Europe and again defeated all comers.

The second phase of their program began at another Gold Coast camp in mid-2003. The interesting shift we witnessed was how newly selected members came to the camp better prepared to be a part of the new Boomers squad. In effect, the plan the players set the previous year had started to take hold. Players who had previously not been involved with the Boomers squad had heard and seen enough to understand that there was a new culture around the team.

The foundation had been laid, but the trick was being disciplined enough not to undermine that foundation.

We had to ensure that the team never indulged in what I call 'retrospective team talk', which is talking about the way things used to be. They had to be able to talk about the team and behave the way they wanted to be now and into the future. Recalling the past causes uncertainty within the team because it confuses people: What are the others thinking? Are we all on the same page? At training, at work, or in any environment where team members were mixing together, they were encouraged to remind one another of the behaviour required of them now, in their preferred state, rather than how they were in the past.

~

ALTHOUGH BRIAN THOUGHT THE basketball culture might struggle with peer reviews the players took to it like ducks to water and soon afterwards I was working with Brian and the Sydney Kings, as well as with the Boomers' assistant coach, Brendan Joyce, who was coaching the Wollongong Hawks in the NBL.

The Kings, it would be fair to say, already had some fairly strong trademarks. The basketball world referred to them as the 'Violet Crumbles' on account of their record of making the play-offs time and again and failing to deliver. They wanted a new trademark and a set of behaviours built around hardness, or mental strength; to, basically, arrest the crumbles.

Brian already had a few trademarks of his own, for developing teams with a strong defensive mindset, physically fit athletes, and people who would willingly play their specified role in a team.

The Kings' captain, Shane Heal, a player with NBA experience and a well-earned reputation for toughness, desperately wanted to break the existing perception of the Kings and replace it with something harder and tougher.

For all Brian's initial misgivings about basketballers' preparedness to accept something like the performance improvement model that he'd first seen in action at Collingwood, the process for the Kings was essentially the same one Central District and St Kilda had used, which was even more demanding of the group than the version of the program we'd run at Collingwood. Like the football clubs, the Kings' involvement in the program doesn't look to have done them any great harm.

Reassuring to me was the fact that when Shane Heal retired his replacement as the Kings' captain, Jason Smith, took on the role in a similar fashion to Shane; tough, hard and uncompromising. I thought it was a good sign that the Kings' culture had become, if you like, sustainable.

Brendan Joyce and the Wollongong Hawks also adopted the principles of the Performance Improvement Program and the Hawks have obtained similar benefits to the other teams using the program. Unfortunately for the Kings and the Hawks, they have to compete against one another and there's only one NBL title on offer.

~

PAUL ROOS PLAYED OVER 350 AFL GAMES before he retired at the end of the 1998 season. He was working as an assistant coach for the Swans in 2002 when the head coach, Rodney Eade, called it a day mid-season and Paul was asked to fill in for the remaining ten games while the club administration pursued experienced AFL coaches.

Whatever plans the club administration might have had for the coach's position, they didn't work out. The team won six of the ten games they played while Paul was in the caretaker role and Swans' supporters rose up en masse and made it clear they thought he was the man for the job.

Paul was, of all the coaches I'd worked with up to that point, probably the most ready to accept the philosophies behind the Performance Improvement Program and surely would have coached along those lines whether I was involved or not. Respect and consideration around the club were not the products of football talent, they had to be earned in other ways.

One of Paul's first addresses to the players after he became head coach was to acknowledge them as individuals: 'You know that old football adage about how when you come to a club we will treat everyone equally?' he said, 'Well, that won't be the case here because you are all different'.

On other occasions he's been quoted in the press as having said that 'football now is about coaching individuals in a team environment', although I'm not sure it's widely recognised just how different that approach is to the NO-'I'-IN-'TEAM' coaching philosophies of the past.

In the early stages of the process at Sydney, as the team was discussing how they thought others might see them as a team, Paul intervened and said there was a consistent view in the media that the team would be going backwards before they went anywhere else and that they would finish somewhere near the bottom of the ladder. Rather than deny that perception, he wanted the players to acknowledge that they weren't seen as a particularly good team and to address this view directly.

The team used those negative perceptions as a springboard to devise their trademark and strategies. So how did they want to be seen?

In the discussion, one of the younger players who knew the club's history raised the fact that club hadn't always been known as 'the Swans' and in the distant past had generally been referred to as the 'the Bloodstained Angels', or 'the Angels', or 'the Bloods'. Sometimes groups struggle with the subtleties of 'branding' but not in this instance and 'the Bloods' were reborn.

The team explored what kind of key words and behaviours would be associated with the Bloods, which were somewhat different to those one might attach to a downy white swan. Among other things, the team agreed that no matter who their opposition was there would be no such thing as an acceptable loss; that no lead was insurmountable; that they would always show courage in the face of adversity; if they did lose a match, it would be treated as a learning opportunity; everyone would take responsibility and wouldn't wait for others to act; that the weight of numbers wins football matches, and for a majority of the players to win their positions they'd have to be more accountable as individuals.

I recall Paul Williams, one of the most experienced players in the team, summarising the whole concept briefly in a team meeting after a loss: 'Boys, we're a blue collar outfit. Everyone turns up ready for work or we don't win.'

When Paul Kelly, Sydney's captain for ten years, retired at the end of the 2002 season, the perception was that leadership would be thin at the Swans for some time to come. How could anyone possibly fill the breach Kel had left?

The team had established a clear trademark and set of behaviours and the next step was to select the leaders against these criteria. Each player was given a sheet with five blank spaces to select up to five players they trusted to model their preferred behaviours and, if required, to challenge team-mates should they fall short of our standards. Each player then announced to the group their selections.

Football coaches usually have some reservations about the PIP leadership structure because it's so unlike anything they've known previously. What happens if a talented player—maybe even our *best* player—doesn't get selected to the leadership group? How will the player react? What will we do then? How will we manage the ensuing fallout?

Adam Goodes and Barry Hall are exceptionally talented footballers who in the normal run of things at a football club would have been elevated into leadership roles by virtue of their athletic abilities. But with many far less talented players being ranked ahead of them according to the Bloods' trademark behaviours, they were not initially selected for the leadership group.

Their response was to ask the group where they needed to improve and what they needed to do differently if they were to be of more value to the team. They listened carefully to that feedback then went away and put their heads down and worked hard to improve in the areas they were seen to be falling short and before too long both players became legitimate and highly valued members of the Bloods' leadership group. But if the team had compromised earlier on and elevated them to the group prematurely, not only would Adam and Barry not be quite the footballers and people that they are today, there would have been significantly less incentive for the other players to buy into the Bloods' trademark.

It was another good lesson for me when the players' clear choice for captain was Stuart Maxfield. For those outside the playing group he wasn't an obvious choice; around thirty years old and a very well-credentialed AFL player with over two hundred games under his belt but rarely mentioned in dispatches as being one of the most talented footballers at the club.

Stuart was, in fact, a tremendous choice for captain. He had what the team needed from their captain, which was to maintain a high level of performance himself and the character to make it clear to other players he expected them to follow suit. If the media view was along the lines of 'Why did they pick this guy?', the players had a clear understanding of the reasons behind their decision and a similarly clear understanding that the criteria the media were using ('star quality') bore no relevance whatsoever to the Bloods' trademark.

What followed was a fascinating test of the decision-making framework the Bloods had agreed to. It's well documented that during the 2005 season, for family reasons, Stuart lived in Melbourne for three days each week.

Some commentators voiced their opinions that there was no way Stuart could continue as captain. Family reasons? Being away from the team for half the week? He was hardly a superstar. How could it be justified?

Paul Roos basically said: 'Stuart alone will decide whether he will continue as captain.' In the meantime the club did everything it could to support him.

In that case you could argue that the club was treating a particular player differently and that in some people's book amounts to favouritism. Which it is. Stuart had earned enough respect over a long period to have earned the right to make his own call on the situation and to be supported in whatever decision he might make. It's not a right that would be extended to just anyone. And that's the difference; he'd earned it. In the traditional football structure talent is favoured over all else. Here, at the Bloods, it was clear that Bloods-like behaviour was favoured over talent.

When consulted, the players had no problem with supporting the club's stand on the captaincy. The players, like the coaches, knew Stuart would put the interests of the team first since that was what led to the team appointing him captain in the first place.

Without a trademark or agreed behaviours, how can there be congruency in any team or organisation's decisions? Had it had been a 'better' player in similar circumstances to those Stuart Maxfield encountered but a player who had chosen to live outside the team's trademark and who looked mainly after themselves, it would have been much more difficult extending to them that kind of flexibility. In Stuart's case, the football club showed care and compassion commensurate with the respect he'd earned according to the team's trademark.

The Sydney Swans took the Performance Improvement Program to another level when it adopted its principles more broadly than developing the trademark behaviours and selecting leaders and the club began to use the Bloods principles to guide recruitment and induction and to develop a congruent exit strategy for bona fide Bloods. Also, the leadership group and the coaching panel met regularly and delivered feedback to one another—which I think strengthened the degree of trust between those two groups—and some tremendous strategies for improvement emanated from those meetings. And because the coaching staff and the senior leadership group are probably the most influential personnel at the club in terms of improving the team's performance and maintaining higher performance levels, the mutual trust and respect between those two groups engendered open lines of communication right throughout the club. No one holds back on offering feedback or raising an issue that's bothering them and that can only have one result; any doubts are quickly addressed so expectations are raised. When expectations are raised, people perform better.

~

WORKING WITH THE WOLLONGONG HAWKS NBL team led my having contact with the National Rugby League club St George Illawarra, which has bases in the Sydney suburb of Kogarah, where the St George Leagues Club is located, and Wollongong.

As St George, the Dragons had been one of the most successful Sydney-based clubs, from 1989 to 1999 making the NRL grand final three times, and again in 1999 as St George Illawarra. But nothing much had happened since, with the team around mid-table, occasionally qualifying for the finals, and wearing constant criticism about underperformance.

I had some discussions with the club's CEO, Peter Doust, and the Dragons' senior coach, Nathan Brown, about what we'd been doing in Australian football and basketball.

Nathan was a different kettle of fish to the coaches I was accustomed to. Only thirty years old when I first met him, he'd suffered a life-threatening spinal-cord injury in a pre-season match in 2001 that ended his playing career at the age of twenty-seven. He was by far the youngest professional coach I'd worked with and he was coaching the highest-profile club in the NRL.

Nathan had played alongside some of the senior players in the team, which presents its own unique issues. The very fine line leaders walk is between being liked by people and being respected in their new role by those same people and that line, for Nathan, was a difficult one to find in his early days as a coach.

The Rugby League culture was also different to what I'd known. The expectations of the players were, I thought, even lower than those I encountered when I first started working with AFL clubs in the mid-90s. The group was keen to learn but so little had been put into their development that they didn't know how much they didn't know about team and player development. It was definitely a greenfields project.

At the first session I ran with the Dragons, Nathan asked me how long I thought I'd need for the session and I said that, generally, three or four hours would be adequate. We could look at the framework and break up into smaller groups ...

It was hard not to notice the concerned look on their faces. A three or four hour session? Could Rugby League players cope with three or four hours?

The challenge, of course, is to make sure it's not boring because if it is, three or four minutes is way too long. If the session engages the players and they're interested in what they are doing, time shouldn't be an issue at all.

As it happened there wasn't a problem, and we've conducted longer sessions since and no one's dozed off or run out the door. Expectations can be high or low and players will generally meet them.

There were other doubts, also similar to those I first encountered around the AFL in 1994–95, about the players wanting to be involved in making plans and setting directions. As with the AFL players, I found that was far from true.

The first test of the leadership group came shortly after we set up the trademark and their agreed behaviours and there was an off-field indiscretion from a senior player that required some disciplinary action.

Typically, in systems that aren't based on player ownership, the punishment for a breach of the team's code of behaviour is left up to the coach and the club administration. Fines or other sanctions are imposed and the other players watch from a distance and wonder, 'Was that fair or appropriate?'

In this case the club did impose its own sanctions on the players. But that wasn't the end of it. Afterwards I sat down with the leadership group and asked what they as leaders were going to do about the breach of their code. How were they going to deal with this player?

One player said, 'Well, I guess someone should talk to him ...'

I said, 'It sounds like it's not going to be you?'

He said he'd prefer it wasn't him. We had a joke about that but it was very clear they still believed it was up to the coach or the club administration or the NRL to wield the stick.

Eventually they decided the leadership group would meet with the player concerned and let him know clearly that *they* saw his behaviour was in conflict with their trademark and agreed behaviours and that they would help him with strategies for improving his behaviour.

That wasn't the last test of the trademark. During the season there were a couple of very public breaches of discipline and the players were left asking 'What do we have to do to deal with this?'

It's a learning process and every time I see a breach of discipline in ranks of Rugby League, I'm reminded of the early days of professionalism in the AFL; young players with limited life skills—having often left school prematurely to enter the system—who are paid extremely well for someone their age and with a lot of time on their hands. While those circumstances persist, player discipline is going to be an ongoing battle for professional sports.

Players' ownership is still at the pioneering stage in Rugby League but I'm confident that as its benefits become clearer with time the players will embrace the notion of leadership, trademark, behaviours and peer evaluations and will want to drive their own system with the same rigour we are seeing in the AFL culture nowadays.

~

WORKING WITH THE SYDNEY KINGS and the Dragons led to my meeting Ewen Mackenzie, coach of the New South Wales Waratahs in, at that stage, the Super 12, the professional Rugby Union competition with teams from South Africa, Australia and New Zealand.

New South Wales has a strong domestic Rugby Union competition and the Waratahs always had a good roster of players but had never delivered on that promise over the nine-year existence of the Super 12, during which time only three teams, Canberra, Auckland and Canterbury had managed to win the title. The words most associated with the Waratahs seemed to be 'perennial underachievers'.

We got underway at the start of the 2005 season when the Waratahs players in the Wallabies national team returned in January from international duties. Relative to the other teams I'd worked with, the Waratahs were probably the most reserved at the beginning of the process, perhaps because they'd been through similar looking exercises and those hadn't done much for them. We started the peer evaluation and put up on the board the key words describing how the team wanted to be seen and the key behaviours that might underpin those words.

For the first peer evaluation we looked at the captain, Chris Whitaker. Chris went out of the room and took with him a sheet of paper to write down how he thought the group would describe him and the sort of things they would ask him to start doing, stop doing or keep doing. Inside, five or six small groups were going through the process of evaluating Chris in those same terms.

The overwhelming message Chris received from the players was that he was deeply respected, he had a strong work ethic, was supportive of other team members, communicated well and encouraged input from other players. That is, his performance was very hard to fault. But there was also a clear message that the other players wanted him to be more assertive as their leader. In short, they thought he could be a bit harder on them and expect more of them.

Without some kind of feedback framework or trademark about how we want to be as a team and the sort of behaviours we expect of one another, it makes it very difficult for a leader to show real leadership because if we've not had the discussion about some kind of agreed code of behaviour, the risk is that when the players are challenged they may well say, 'Well, since when did we have to be like you?' It doesn't even have to happen; the risk of it happening can be enough to see the leader fall back on their own personal standards and, without making express demands on the players, simply hope the others will follow their positive example.

Chris had latent assertion skills that only needed a setting where he could hear clearly that it was okay for him to go ahead and use them. And of all the leaders I've dealt with, Chris was probably the fastest to grasp the concepts behind trademarks and behaviours and how they apply in practice. In a very short time he began to drive the peer evaluation process and made my presence largely redundant.

The Waratahs operated within the framework without fear or favour, whether it was a senior international or one of the younger players just entering their system. The players were honest and upfront with one another from the outset of the process and they leapt straight over hurdles some teams had baulked at for months and longer. As the issues clarified themselves, other senior players began to weigh in and get behind Chris to support the process and Phil Waugh in particular helped enormously by sharing leadership responsibilities.

It's still early days at the Waratahs but I believe there have been some significant positive signs that suggest the team will become a formidable combination. That has already been reflected in some very solid performances during 2005 when the team was still in the early stages of their Performance Improvement Program, and experience says the real benefits, the long-term ones that see a team maintaining a consistent high standard of performance, don't kick in for at least a couple of years. But as St Kilda and Collingwood in the AFL, and the Kings and the Boomers proved, there's no rule that says a team has to hold back until the third year of the program to shake their 'underachiever' tag.

LOOKING FORWARD, LOOKING BACK

IT SEEMS LIKE JUST THE OTHER DAY that I sat down with Alan Stewart to talk about whether the leadership and teamwork principles we were devising in the air force might help a struggling football club. On the other hand, so much has happened since, as Alan describes it, 'two fools collided', that our first meeting can also seem like several lifetimes ago. I was very lucky to have met someone like Alan with the courage to support the program when there was no evidence whatsoever to suggest it might actually work.

It's less of a faith-based argument nowadays, now that some results are in. After Alan left Central District they became regular finalists until, in 2000, with Peter Jonas coaching the team, they won the club's first-ever SANFL premiership. They were premiers again in 2001, runners-up in 2002, and then premiers in 2003, 2004 and 2005. As we wrote on the piece of paper that we attached to the gum tree a decade ago, above else all they wanted to be respected. That they certainly are.

Gerard Fitzgerald took the Performance Improvement Program with him on his coaching journey from country clubs to North Ballarat, Springvale and Port Melbourne in the Victorian Football League, and as the Victorian State Football League representative team coach. He's currently coaching elite junior footballers at the North Ballarat Rebels in the TAC Cup competition.

The Sydney Kings were NBL champions in 2003, 2004 and 2005, the latter in a play-off against the Wollongong Hawks. Both teams are highly respected units, as are the Boomers, who continue to punch above their weight.

We began work at the Adelaide Crows when Neil Craig took over there near the end of the 2004 season. Neil had played in the SANFL but before he took up coaching was probably more widely known as the sports scientist from the South Australian Sports Institute who'd helped Malcolm Blight guide the team to consecutive premierships in 1997 and 1998. One of the coaching staff at Adelaide probably summed it up, saying Neil saw 'football culture' as an excuse for not pursuing excellence.

Parts of the Australian football establishment regarded Neil as an outsider due to his lack of AFL coaching experience, and the media misread the situation again, with some commentators loudly proclaiming that Adelaide's playing and coaching stocks would see the team finish outright last in 2005 and a long way off the pace for many seasons to come. The Crows finished the 2005 season on top of the ladder and then made it through to a preliminary final, which, the commentators agreed, wasn't a bad effort for a coach in his first full season as coach and 'still learning the ropes'. At this stage it looks like Neil is going to take the Performance Improvement Program to a new level.

The St George Illawarra Dragons, in the second year of their Performance Improvement Program, made it through to a preliminary final in 2005. The Waratahs, in their first year of the program, made it through to the 2005 Super 12 grand final. If those results seem rather immediate, the real benefits of the clubs' cultural changes won't become fully apparent until the third year of the program (and beyond).

The Sydney Swans make for a more conventional story, taking a few years to grow into the program. They were criticised throughout 2005 for their style of play—even the AFL's CEO had a shot, complaining that the team's approach would lose more games than it would win—but they persevered anyway, then waged one of the more noteworthy AFL finals campaigns in recent times that earned the club its first premiership since 1933.

~

ONE JOURNALIST OBSERVED OF THE AFL teams engaged in the program that '... when they emerge from these confronting sessions and the season progresses, the miracle is that they kick and mark and handpass better'. It's no miracle and it's repeatable. Substantial performance improvements are available to *any* team that develops an environment where its members have a vested interest in their colleagues' development and they individually and collectively drive themselves towards being the team they've agreed they want to be. Other synergies come into play when a group truly behaves as a team and that's when one plus one can begin to look like three or, on a really good day, maybe even four or five.

Advances in sports science have made enormous contributions to athletes' physical conditioning—the mechanics, if you like—and there is a broadening recognition that the next frontier for significant performance improvements is in the teamwork, or dynamics. As I write this, six of the sixteen Australian Football League clubs have adopted the Performance Improvement Program.

In Australia, probably due to our isolation and relatively small population, we've managed to avoid many of the excesses of professional sport that have seen the 'team' concept all but disappear. But as we've seen, with dynamics closing the gap on mechanics, 'all-star' teams aren't delivering the guaranteed outcomes they might have in the past, the most glaring example of that being the US basketball team's performance at the 2004 Athens Olympics.

As the old saying about a champion team beating a team of champions continues to sink in, expect to see a continuing shift of emphasis in recruiting for elite team sports from simply identifying the most athletically gifted individuals available to more subtle recruiting criteria where an individual's capacity to learn and develop into an effective team member are valued as much as their athletic talents. And that, along with a broadening recognition that a person who thinks better of themselves will ultimately be a better player, suggests to me that sport—having justifiably stood accused at times of tolerating or promoting undesirable behaviour—will have an increasingly positive story to tell in the future. Forget arguments about athletes being role models and presenting them with sets of commandments to follow; for athletes to have a vested interest in the issue they only need to understand how their behaviour links to their self-image and how that in turn links to their sporting performance.

Alongside the Australian football, Rugby League, Rugby Union and basketball teams using the PIP framework, an increasing number of businesses and educational facilities are adopting the model to achieve congruency between their team's goals and their behaviour. How much better those teams are for using the framework than they would have been otherwise is hard to gauge. Teams and organisations that find success while using the program aren't evidence of anything in particular but their successes do say, I think, that trying to achieve congruency between a team's goals and its behaviour doesn't do the team any harm.

One of the program's strengths has always been its simplicity and with evolution it has become, paradoxically, increasingly simple. Nowadays it's a remarkably user-friendly performance improvement tool for any given team in any given environment. We've derived from user feedback all sorts of lists and diagrams and templates that can be applied to all kinds of situations, none of which will appear here because I've learned to leave it up to our athlete facilitators to make sense of the data. They've promised me that one day they're going to put it all down in a book in language I can understand.

Tibetan Buddhists reckon that if the student is not better than the teacher then the teacher has failed. In that regard I'm going okay. Nowadays my boss is Craig Biddiscombe, a former AFL footballer who joined Leading Teams as an athlete facilitator and developed his skills until, as our peer evaluations revealed, his surpassed mine.

How's Your Team Going?

THERE ARE NO SHORTCUTS to good leadership and teamwork but diagnosing the problems doesn't take long at all. You can do it yourself.

How would your team describe itself? Is that congruent with what you want?

What behaviours do you tolerate in your team that you know are counter-productive? Listen carefully to the people around you. Do you hear the language of responsibility? Or the language of blame and excuses? Does your team's culture harbour any deep-seated excuses for poor performance?

Who are the real leaders in your organisation? What gets noticed in your organisation? Why?

Is feedback given in your team? Is it honest? Is it done face-to-face? How do the recipients respond?

What are the consequences for non-compliance with trademark behaviours? Who are the custodians of those standards?

There's your answer.